REAL STORIES
FOR THE SOUL

REAL STORIES

FOR THE SOUL

THOMAS NELSON PUBLISHERS
Nashville, Tennessee

The Author and Publisher sincerely appreciate all those whose stories are retold or quoted in this book. We have made every effort to quote the source for each story. If we have inadvertently left anyone out, please let us know.

Published in Nashville, Tennessee, by Thomas Nelson, Inc.

Scripture quotations are from the NEW KING JAMES VERSION of the Bible © 1982 by Thomas Nelson Publishers.

Library of Congress Cataloging-in-Publication Data

Morgan, Robert J., 1952–
    Real stories for the soul / by Robert J. Morgan
        p.   cm.
    ISBN 0-7852-4516-2
    1. Christian biography.   I. Title.
BR1700.2.M658   2000
242—dc21   00–041112
                                                          CIP

Printed in the United States of America
1 2 3 4 5 6 — 05 04 03 02 01 00

Preface

Some people collect baseball cards or butterflies. I collect stories. My father was a great storyteller, and perhaps I owe a lot of it to him. My mom is pretty good at it, too—especially when describing her early life in the Appalachians. But I'm also indebted to a lady in North Carolina who, twenty-five years ago, suggested I begin "the notebook habit."

In the years since, I've jotted down hundreds of stories in my little notebook, along with clippings, quotes, and observations. They've been endlessly recycled into sermons, after-dinner talks, banquet speeches, and books. Best of all, they've helped a retiring soul like me survive in social settings.

Stories do all those things and more. They communicate truth and help us see the nuts-and-bolts of God's wonderful lessons. They entertain and inspire. They can even convict and convert. No wonder Charles Spurgeon, the 18th century Prince of Preachers, used to tell his ministerial students, "Don't forget to give them a few anecdotes."

So here are 101 anecdotes which, when leisurely read and enjoyed, will provide a liberal handful of antidotes for the ills of life.

My deepest thanks and appreciation go to Phil Stoner and Teri Wilhelms of Thomas Nelson Publishers for their vision and encouragement.

And to you, for adding these stories to your own collection.

TO:

Steve, Ann, Sara,
and John

His Father's Voice

꧁

He was only forty-five when the doctor told him he was dying. Sitting in stunned silence, Jonathan Thigpen of Wheaton, Illinois, tried to focus his gyrating mind on Dr. O'Riley's matter-of-fact diagnosis. Amyotrophic Lateral Sclerosis. ALS. Lou Gehrig's Disease. A cruel, incurable illness characterized by progressive muscular weakness resulting in paralysis and death. Fifty percent of all ALS patients die within eighteen months of diagnosis. The cause is unknown, and there is no cure. It is always terminal. Perhaps a year; two at most.

But it couldn't be. This wasn't part of the plan. Jonathan was relatively young and happily married. His daughter was in high school, and he himself was working on his doctorate. As head of the Evangelical Training Association he was providing Christian Education materials for churches and schools around the world.

Perhaps a year? Two at most?

Jonathan later recalled, *I remember walking out of the doctor's office in Carol Stream, Illinois, and deep in the pit of my stomach there was a feeling of overwhelming fear. I can' t describe it other than it felt like I was being hugged by something so dark and so horrible that I can't describe it.*

Just before the darkness totally engulfed him, he heard a familiar voice speaking distinctly in his mind. Jonathan was a preacher's kid, and, growing up, he had noticed that every night after supper his dad would disappear for an hour or two. For many years, Jonathan didn't know where his father went. But one day his dad invited him to tag along, and from then on they spent their early evenings visiting the hospitals together. At every stop Dr. Thigpen would chat briefly with the patient, smile, ask concerned questions, then pull out his little New Testament and Psalms.

Time after time, Jonathan had listened as his dad had read from Psalm 46:

> *God is our refuge and strength,*
> *A very present help in trouble.*
> *Therefore we will not fear,*
> *Even though the earth be removed,*

And though the mountains be carried
into the midst of the sea.

Now in the worst moment of Jonathan's life, the
voices of his earthly father and of his Heavenly Father
united in the chambers of his memory, and those words
reverberated in nearly audible fashion through his mind.
The effect was electric.

By the time I got to my car that cloud of darkness had
begun to lift because I realized that God was still in control. I
didn't have any more answers than I had had when I was in
the doctor's office five minutes before, but I can tell you this: Fear
cannot stand in the face of a faith and a God who does not
change. My fear had left.

In the months that followed, Jonathan's body weakened but
his spirit grew stronger as he traveled across the country sharing
Psalm 46, imparting strength to fellow-sufferers, and reminding
his listeners of our refuge and strength—a God who is a very
present help in trouble. ❧

The Hand That Rocks the Cradle

❧❦❧

Hers was a difficult life. She was the twenty-fifth child in a dissenter's family in a harsh age. Though brilliant, she procured little education. Though strong-willed, she lived in a male-dominated period. She married an older man and bore him nineteen children, nine of whom died in infancy. Her house burned up, her barn fell down, her health failed, and she lived with the wolf at the door. In the end several of her children bitterly disappointed her.

But two of her children changed the world.

She was Susanna Annesley, born in London in 1669. Twenty years later, she married an Anglican clergyman named Samuel Wesley, and they were assigned the pastorate of a church in the dreary little town of Epworth, England. There they served forty years, enduring hardships like these:

- Samuel's salary was so small (and he was so incapable of managing it) that he was thrown into debtor's prison, leaving Susanna to fend for herself.

- He was an unpopular minister, aloof and severe with his congregation, resulting in rejection and even persecution. On one occasion, the Wesley home was burned to the ground, almost taking the Wesleys with it.

- Samuel and Susanna were both strong-willed and argumentative. Samuel once prayed for the king and waited for Susanna's "Amen." She didn't say it. "I do not believe the Prince of Orange to be the king," she said spiritedly. "Then you and I must part," replied Samuel "for if we have two kings we must have two beds." They separated, to be reunited only after the king's death.

- They also disagreed about Susanna's ministry, for her Bible lessons drew more listeners than his sermons, causing Samuel intense feelings of resentment.

- Susanna gave birth to a daughter during the election of 1705. The nurse, exhausted by overnight revelry, slept so heavily the next morning that she rolled on the baby and smothered it.

- Susanna herself was often bedfast, having to delegate

home duties to the children. But several of her children were so wayward that she called them "a constant affliction."

- Her brother, having promised her a sizable gift, disappeared mysteriously and was never heard from again.
- Finally, on July 21, 1731, Susanna described an accident in which her horses stampeded, throwing Samuel from their wagon and injuring him so that he was never well from that day.

A difficult life. And yet . . .

And yet the parsonage at Epworth was destined to become the most celebrated in English history, for from it came two of the greatest evangelists of all time, John and Charles Wesley. And the mother who raised them shook the world.

Ours is sometimes a difficult life, and we occasionally wonder if we're doing any good. Do our feeble efforts count for eternity? But God has given us a promise, so we press through the difficulty by faith: "Therefore, my beloved brethren, be steadfast, immovable, always abounding in the work of the Lord, knowing that your labor is not in vain in the Lord" (1 Corinthians 15:58). ๛

3

Branch Rickey

❦

Branch Rickey, a member of Baseball's Hall of Fame and long-time manager of several major league teams, was a Christian. Once while head of the old Brooklyn Dodgers, he attended negotiations involving a ballplayer's contract. But in the middle of the meeting, to everyone's surprise, Rickey threw down his pencil, pushed back his chair, and growled, "The deal's off."

"Why?" asked the astonished men. "We're coming along well with these negotiations."

"Because," said Rickey, "you've been talking about a friend of mine, and I don't like it."

"But what friend do you mean? We haven't been talking about anyone, let alone a friend of yours."

"Oh, yes, you have," replied Rickey. "You've mentioned him in almost every sentence." And he referred them to their constant profane use of the name of Jesus Christ.

The men quickly apologized, and the negotiations continued, minus the profanity. ᎒᠍ᕀ

4

The One-Eyed Soldier

❦

Thomas Webb was a portly, homely, ragged, patched-up fireball who helped establish Methodism in America. Born in England, Webb had initially chosen a soldier's career and had fought with the British army in 1759. He was wounded and returned to England, only to be retired on captain's pay. About 1764, he was converted to Christ in Bristol under the preaching of John Wesley, and he soon began applying his military mind in the Methodist campaign for souls. He became an ardent preacher in England and Ireland; then in 1766, he came to America as a soldier for Christ.

In New York City, Captain Webb fired up a discouraged preacher named Philip Embury, assisting him in preaching the Gospel. New York's population was only about fifteen thousand people, and few envisioned its becoming a great city. But Webb saw the potential and joined several others in constructing a small chapel, forty-two by sixty, with a seating capacity of seven hundred. It was built of stone, covered with blue plaster. The benches had no backs. Candles provided light. It was a plain building, but worshippers claimed it had "the beauty of Holiness." The John Street Church, the first Methodist Chapel in New York City, has been called "The Mother Church of Methodism in America."

Afterward, Captain Webb traveled far and wide—to Long Island, Philadelphia, Baltimore, Delaware, Jamaica, Europe. And during his periodic stops in England, he continually urged Wesley to send more preachers to the colonies.

Those who met Webb never forgot him, chiefly because of his dangling sword and the large, green oversized patch that covered his left eye, war wounds from the Battle of Louisburg (1759). It was described this way:

A ball hit him on the bone which guards the right eye, and taking an oblique direction, burst the eyeball, and passing through his palate into his mouth, he swallowed it. A comrade said, "He is dead enough." Webb replied, "No, I am not dead." In three months, he was able to rejoin his comrades. He was never ashamed of his scars.

Neither was the Apostle Paul, who once wrote: "I

bear in my body the marks of the Lord Jesus" (Galatians 6:17). How marvelous that God even uses our misfortunes for His glory, and He makes all things work together for good (Romans 8:28)! ઌ

5

Over the Falls

❧

On July 9, 1960, Roger Woodward, age seven, and his seventeen-year-old sister Deanna, went for a boat ride. They were guests of Jim Honeycutt, a friend from Niagara Falls, New York, who took them out on the Niagara River, somewhere above the falls.

The fun stopped when the boat developed motor trouble and the current began carrying them downstream. As Jim struggled to start the engine, they began wobbling in the choppy water, and the boat suddenly capsized, catapulting all three into the river.

Jim was instantly swept away and, in a moment of horror, flew over the falls and was killed, his body washing ashore four days later. Deanna was plucked from the river about twenty feet from the edge of the Falls by two tourists from New Jersey.

But Roger, wearing only swimming trunks and an

orange life preserver, was too far from the banks of the river to be rescued. Thrashing frantically in the current, he saw the spray from the falls rushing toward him, but he was helpless to stop himself or even to slow down. As horrified passers-by watched, he plunged through water and mist and air, caught in the thunderous power of the Canadian Horseshoe Falls, toppling downward, head over heels, into the abyss.

The "Maid of the Mist" tourist boat was just turning away from the Falls when the crew spotted a tiny orange speck, bobbing in the basin of the falls. Closer inspection revealed a stunned, crying boy. Workers pulled Roger from the water, and he was rushed to the hospital where he remained three days with a slight concussion before being released.

Thirty years passed and Roger Woodward returned to Niagara Falls to give his testimony at the Glengate Alliance Church. The audience was hushed as he told his miraculous story, the panic he felt as he drifted helplessly toward the precipice, the anger he felt because no one on the shoreline could help him, the flashbacks he experienced as he inwardly said goodbye to his parents and his dog and his toys.

"It wasn't the hand of fate (that saved me)," he told

the church. "It wasn't the hand of luck. It was the Spirit of the Living God that saved my life that day and saved my sister and gave us hope that one day we could come to know Him." ॐ

6

The Bullets of God

◈

The old Lutheran Church in Du Bois, Pennsylvania, seemed an unlikely place for the squirming Thompson kid on a stuffy Sunday night long ago. He was disinterested, bored, nerves ready to explode. But a thought suddenly hit him like a bullet: *Some day you are going to preach from that pulpit.*

He shook off the thought, and as the days passed he almost forgot the vivid impression he had received that Sunday night.

Entering adolescence, W. F. Thompson lost all interest in church. Other less noble, more appealing activities drew his attention, and Trinity Lutheran Church became a faded memory.

At age seventeen, Thompson joined the Marines and emerged from boot camp a savage fighter. He seized the violence of war like an alcoholic grabbing a bottle. He craved blood. "In combat, I enjoyed killing," he recalled, "especially with a bayonet."

After the war, Thompson moved to Raleigh, North Carolina, where he went into business. One Friday a man entered his office and, brandishing a gun, demanded money from the firm's safe. Thompson's fingers curled around an imaginary bayonet. Every fiber in him itched to tackle the gunman, but the danger to others was too great.

Suddenly a customer entered the room, and the thief, unnerved, darted away. Thompson pursued him out of the building and down the street. As he turned the corner onto Fayetteville Street, he came upon the gunman, who was poised, waiting for him, revolver in hand. The first bullet hit Thompson in the chest. The next two struck his left shoulder and arm.

Thompson clung to life through the weekend, but on Monday the doctors gently urged his wife to call the undertaker. "He has only a few moments left," they said. Friends gathered by his bed, and every breath appeared his last. But W.F. Thompson lingered, unconscious, clinging to life. At length, he opened his eyes and glanced about the room, trying to remember who and where he was. He spied a Bible open on the bedside table, a Gideon New

Testament. Its presence angered him. Reaching over with a groan, he closed it and sank back into a stupor. The next time he opened his eyes he saw the New Testament opened as before. He managed to slam it shut before collapsing again.

When his eyes jerked open the third time, they involuntarily darted to his bedside table. The Book open again, waiting to be read. Summoning his strength, he reached over with grunt, seized it with his good arm, and prepared to hurl it across the room. But as the Bible hovered above his head, it pages opened to John 6, and the words of verse 37 hit him like a hail of bullets: *All that the Father gives Me will come to Me; and the one who comes to me I will by no means cast out.*

With trembling hands, he opened the page more carefully and read the verse again, the again and again. "Does this mean me?" he asked aloud.

"Especially you," the Lord whispered to his heart.

And *that* is the message W. F. Thompson later shared when he preached his first sermon at the old Trinity Lutheran Church in Du Bois, Pennsylvania. 🙿

The Woman Who Saw an Angel

❦

Years ago, I popped into a hotel elevator and found myself standing beside the famous Christian writer and Nazi death-camp survivor, Corrie Ten Boom. I recognized her at once, having read her books and seen her on television. When I introduced myself, instead of giving me a usual greeting she squinted at me as only an old woman can squint and asked with Dutch accent: "Young man, have you ever seen an angel?"

"No," I replied, startled, "Not that I know of."

"Well, I have," she declared. And in the time our elevator took to reach the bottom floor, she told me of a time when she was smuggling Bibles into Communist Eastern Europe. The border guard was checking everyone's luggage, and she knew her load of Bibles would surely be discovered. In alarm she prayed, "Lord, you have said that you would watch over your Word. Now, please watch over your Word that I am smuggling."

Suddenly as she looked at her suitcase, it seemed to glow with light. No one else saw it; but to her it was unmistakable. There was a aura of light wrapped around that suitcase.

Her turn came at customs, and the guard, who had so vigilantly opened and inspected every piece of everyone's luggage, glanced at her bags, shrugged, and waved her through.

It was an angel, she told me, who had helped her deliver God's Word behind the Iron Curtain. ❧

The Disease of Me

❧§❧

Basketball coach Pat Riley in his book *The Winner Within* tells about the 1980 World Championship Los Angeles Lakers. They won the NBA Championship that year, and they were recognized as the best basketball team in the world. They began their 1980–1981 season considered likely to win back-to-back championships. But within weeks of the season opener, Magic Johnson tore the cartilage in his knee, and needed a three-month recuperation period.

The team and the fans rallied, and the remaining players played their hearts out. They determined to make it through that period without losing their rankings. They were winning seventy percent of their games when the time began to draw near for Magic Johnson to return to action.

As his return grew closer, the publicity surrounding

him increased. During time-outs at the games, the public address announcer would always say, "And don't forget to mark your calendars for February 27th. Magic Johnson returns to the lineup of your World Champion Los Angeles Lakers!" During that announcement, the other players would look up and curse. They'd say, "We're winning *now*. What's so great about February 27th."

As the day approached, fewer and fewer things were written or said about the players who were putting out so much effort. All the media attention was focused on the one player who hadn't been doing a thing. Finally the 27th came, and as they clicked through the turnstiles every one of the 17,500 ticket holders was handed a button that said, "The Magic Is Back!"

At least fifty press photographers crowded onto the floor while the players were introduced. Normally only the starters were introduced, and Magic Johnson was going to be on the bench when the game began. But he was nevertheless included in the introductions. At the mention of his name, the arena rocked with a standing ovation. Flashbulbs went off like popcorn. Magic Johnson was like a returning god to the crowd that night.

Meanwhile the other players who had carried the team for three months and who were totally ignored, were seething with jealousy, resentment, anger, and envy. They were so resentful that they barely won the game that night against a bottom-of-the-bucket team, and eventually the morale of the entire team collapsed. The players turned on each other. The coach was fired. And they eventually lost their opening series of the play-offs, having one of the most disastrous records ever.

"Because of greed, pettiness, and resentment," Riley later said, "we executed one of the fastest falls from grace in NBA history. It was the Disease of Me." ⋟

The Moon Shall Not Give Its Light

❧§§❧

When you seek to share your faith in Christ, remember that God has gone before you, preparing the heart of your listener, just a a diligent farmer plows and prepares the ground in which he intends to sow his seed.

When Bible translator Jim Walton first entered the primeval jungles of La Sabana in Columbia, South America, he thought no one there had previously heard the Gospel.

Then he met Andres.

Andres was the oldest son of Chief Fernando of the Muinane tribe, and by occupation a tapper of latex from rubber trees. He lived three days from La Sabana, and he tended about two hundred rubber trees over a one-hundred-acre section of jungle. Andres had been asking himself questions about life—where we came from, what happens after death—but had found no satisfying answers.

One night in boredom, Andres had begun fiddling with a transistor radio given him by a rubber baron. Suddenly he picked up a sharp, clear signal from Trans World Radio in Bonaire. A man was reading these words: "The sun (shall) be darkened, and the moon shall not give her light, and the stars shall fall from heaven, and the powers of the heavens shall be shaken: And then shall appear the sign of the Son of man coming in the clouds of heaven. . . ."

By strange coincidence, that very evening the moon did not give its light. Though Andres didn't understand it at the time, a total lunar eclipse had covered the entire jungle with blackness. The young Colombian was deeply stirred.

Andres soon returned home, and the next day Jim Walton arrived unexpectedly and, opening his New Testament in front of Chief Fernando's guest house, began to read. Andres was spellbound.

When I saw you reading that book, I knew it was the book from the radio, the book that had the truth. And when you said it was God's Word, and you wanted to put it in my language, I determined to help you.

He did help. For the next eighteen years, Andres served Jim as co-translator, helping him complete the first draft of the New Testament and portions of the Old Testament in the language of the Muinane people. ❧

Why Not Cuss?

❦

I have a friend in jail, a sixteen-year-old who was convicted of assault with a deadly weapon. Since being in jail, he has given his life to Christ, and nothing has pleased me more than watching him grow in the Lord. He has been reading his Bible each day, praying, witnessing to his fellow inmates, and trying to clean up his old habits.

The one he's had the most trouble with has been his profanity. The other day as I visited with him behind bars, he brought up his cussing. Every once in a while, he admitted, a profane word flies out of his mouth.

"Give me an example," I told him. "Go ahead and cuss for me." He seemed shocked that I would suggest such a thing, but I insisted. "Let'er fly," I told him.

"I can't do that," he said with embarrassment.

"Sure you can. Go ahead and let loose."

"I'm not going to do it," he said. "I can't."

I kept pressing him, but when I saw that I couldn't get a single cuss word out of him, I asked him why he was being so stubborn about it. "Why are you refusing to do what I ask?"

"Because you're my pastor," he said. "I can't cuss in front of you."

Exactly.

"If you're ashamed to cuss in my presence," I asked, staring him straight in the eye, "why is it that you aren't ashamed to cuss in the Lord's presence? He is always with you in your cell. He's always present at your side."

The young man got my point, and he hasn't cussed since.

If we were to visualize God's presence as it really is, it would be both a comfort to our hearts and a restraint to our behavior.

Brother Lawrence wrote: _When we are faithful to keep ourselves in His holy presence and set Him always before us, this not only hinders our offending Him and doing anything that may displease Him . . . but it also begets in us a holy freedom, and, if I may so speak, a familiarity with God, wherewith we ask, and that successfully, the graces we stand in need of._ ❧

Why Should It Be Thought Incredible?

❦

Whatever our philosophy or theology, everyone has moments when we doubt our beliefs and believe our doubts. Even Christians occasionally ask, "Is the Gospel really true?" Anticipating that, Jesus gave us a massive amount of evidence for the veracity of His resurrection and provided "many infallible proofs" that He had indeed risen bodily from the grave (Acts 1:3). It reassures us to know that these "proofs" have convinced even the unlikeliest of skeptics.

Albert L. Roper was a prominent Virginia attorney, a graduate of the University of Virginia and its law school, who eventually became mayor of the city of Norfolk. He once began a thorough legal investigation into the evidence for the resurrection of Christ, asking himself the question: Can any intelligent person accept the resurrection story? After examining the evidence at length, he came away asking a different question: Can any intelligent person deny the weight of this evidence?

One of the most interesting books in my library was written by a man who set out to disprove the resurrection of Jesus Christ. He was an English journalist named Frank Morison who viewed Christianity with disfavor, deciding that if he could prove that Christ's resurrection was a mere myth, he could debunk all of Christianity.

He poured over the evidence, absorbing all the information he could and marshaling all his arguments. Not only was he unable to disprove the resurrection, but he was compelled on the weight of the evidence to become a Christian himself.

And his book? It is a powerful argument in favor of the resurrection, called *Who Moved The Stone?* It is ". . . essentially a confession," Morison says, "the inner story of a man who originally set out to write one kind of book and found himself compelled by the sheer force of circumstances to write quite another."

Josh McDowell entered university as a young man looking for a good time and searching for happiness and meaning in life. He tried going to church, but found religion unsatisfying. He ran for student leadership positions, but was disappointed by how quickly the glamour wore off. He tried the party circuit, but he woke up Monday mornings feeling worse than ever.

He finally noticed a group of students engaged in Bible study, and he became intrigued by the radiance of one of the young ladies. He asked her a reason for it. She looked him straight in the eye, smiled, and said, "Jesus Christ."

"Oh, for heaven's sake," he retorted, "don't give me that garbage about religion."

She replied, "I didn't say religion; I said Jesus Christ."

The students invited him to intellectually examine the claims of Christ and the evidence for Christianity. He accepted their challenge, and after much study and research, finally admitted that he couldn't refute the body of proof supporting Christianity. McDowell received Christ as his Savior, and his research became the background for his book *Evidence That Demands A Verdict*.

One of the major factors in his conversion to Christianity was his inability to ignore the historical resurrection of Jesus Christ, a point he made later to a student at the University of Uruguay who asked him, "Professor Mc-Dowell, why can't you intellectually refute Christianity?"

"For a very simple reason," replied McDowell. "I am not able to explain away an event in history—the resurrection of Jesus Christ."

Years ago in England, two men set out to disprove Christianity. One was a well-known English jurist and literary scholar named Lord Littleton. The other was Gilbert West. They agreed that if Christianity was to be discredited, two things were necessary: to disprove the resurrection and to explain the conversion of Saul of Tarsus in a way that satisfied the skeptics. The two men divided these tasks between themselves, Lord Littleton taking the problem of Saul of Tarsus and Gilbert West agreeing to research the resurrection. They invested over a year for their studies, then met together again to compare notes. Each one was astonished to discover that the other had become a Christian.

Lew Wallace was a famous general and literary genius of the 19th century who, along with his friend Robert Ingersoll, decided to write a book that would forever destroy "the myth of Christianity." For two years, Wallace studied in the libraries of Europe and America, then he started his book. But while writing the second chapter, he found himself on his knees crying out to Jesus Christ in the words of Thomas who had himself once doubted the resurrection of Jesus Christ: "My Lord and my God."

The book he was writing became the great novel about the times of Christ, *Ben Hur.*

"Why should it be thought incredible by you," the Apostle Paul once asked, "that God raises the dead?" ಸ

Turn That Over to Me

❧❧❧

Brain fatigue, nervous exhaustion, near collapse, depression. . . . Those were the terms Methodist missionary Stanley Jones used to describe his deteriorating condition. He had gone to India with visionary passion, but his energy had evaporated amid unbearable heat, hostility, and anxiety. He felt himself unraveling.

His doctor prescribed a year's rest in America, but he collapsed aboard ship while trying to speak at a Sunday morning service at sea and barely made it home. Once there, Jones tried to rest, but his nerves crackled like a short-circuiting electrical connection. He insisted on returning to India a year later, but he no sooner landed in Bombay than he collapsed again and was sent to the mountains for several more months of rest and relaxation. Finally returning to work, Jones quickly used up his meager emotional reserves and was plunged again into depression and debilitation. Friends feared for his life.

It was in this state that Jones traveled to the city of Lucknow to conduct a series of meetings. There one night while praying, he suddenly felt the Lord speaking to him. Though not audible, the Lord's voice almost seemed so. Jones sensed these words: *Are you yourself ready for this work to which I have called you?*

"No, Lord, I am done for," Jones replied. "I have reached the end of my resources."

If you will turn that over to Me and not worry about it, I will take care of it.

"Lord," Jones said, "I close the bargain right here."

At that moment, E. Stanley Jones later said, a great peace settled into his heart and pervaded his whole being. "I knew it was done! Life—Abundant Life—had taken possession of me. I was so lifted up that I scarcely touched the road as I quietly walked home that night. Every inch was holy ground. For days after that I hardly knew I had a body. I went through the days, working far into the night, and came down to bedtime wondering why in the world I should ever go to bed at all, for there was not the slightest trace of tiredness of any kind. I seemed possessed by life and peace and rest—by Christ Himself."

Jones labored on for decades, serving over forty years in India, preaching around the world—sometimes three times a day, writing a dozen books, and becoming one of the most famous missionaries of his generation.

From his evening encounter with the Lord at Lucknow until his death in January, 1973, E. Stanley Jones lived in the glow of the sufficiency of Christ Himself, never forgetting the Lord's promise, *If you turn that over to Me and not worry about it, I will take care of it.* ॐ

13

The Overflow Principle

❦

Wat happens when preachers, speakers, and teachers run short of time? What should we do when we have time for either our private devotions or our lesson preparation, but not both?

On those occasions, wise servants remember Psalm 23:5: *My cup runs over.* Effective ministry is merely the overflow of our personal appointments with the Lord. He's more concerned for our walk with Him than our work with Him. If we guard the former, He'll take care of the latter. To put it differently we're either pipelines or we're just puddles.

Missionary author Isobel Kuhn learned this while a student at Moody Bible Institute. She was invited to give a devotional message during her Junior-Senior party, but she was running short of time. It finally boiled down to a half-hour at supper, and Isobel was faced with a choice: Should she go down and eat at mealtime? Should she skip supper and try to prepare her devotional message? Should she put God first and give that half-hour to Him?

The bell rang, and her roommates left for the dining hall. For a moment, Isobel wavered, but then she threw herself on her knees, overcome with fatigue, and whispered, "Lord, I choose You!" A sense of God's presence lifted her spirits and seemed to restore her strength. As she half knelt, half lay there by her bed, praying and meditating, certain thoughts came to her mind, devotional truths for her own soul took shape.

She later recalled, _Quietly, but point by point, He outlined for me the devotional message I needed to close that evening's program. It was an unforgettable experience and an unforgettable lesson._

When time came to leave the room, she slipped into the party, and at the end of a Dutch scene, she shared the simple message God had given her. It seemed perfectly appropriate to the occasion and much needed. _Such a hush came over that festive scene that I knew He had spoken, and I was content._

Twenty years passed, Isobel made a return visit to Moody Bible Institute while on furlough from her work in China.

As it happened, it was the day of the Junior-Senior party. As she toured her alma mater, she heard one of the workers say, "One Junior-Senior party stands out in my memory. I forget who led it but it was a Dutch scene and the devotional message blessed my soul. I've never forgotten it."

I was thrilled through and through, Isobel later wrote. *Of course I did not spoil it by telling her who led that devotional. In God's perfect working, the instrument is forgotten. It is the blessing of Himself that is remembered.* ❧

14

Making Friends

The best thing I've ever read about friendship is Proverbs 18:24: *A man who has friends must himself be friendly.*

The second best thing is this quote from Dale Carnegie: *You can make more friends in two months by becoming interested in other people than you can in two years by trying to get other people interested in you.*

Sam Rayburn, democratic leader from Texas, served for more than forty-eight years in the U.S. House of Representatives (1913½61), including seventeen years as speaker. At the height of his career, he was one of the most powerful men in the world, but he never outgrew his friends.

One night, a friend's teenage daughter passed away. Early the next morning the man heard a knock on his door and when he opened it, there was Mr. Rayburn standing outside.

"I just came by to see what I could do to help," said Rayburn.

"I don't think there is anything you can do, Mr. Speaker," said the broken father. "We are making all the arrangements."

"Well," Mr. Rayburn said, "have you had your coffee this morning?"

The man replied that they had not taken time for breakfast. So Mr. Rayburn said that he could at least make coffee for them. While he was working in the kitchen, the man came in and said, "Mr. Speaker, I thought you were supposed to be having breakfast at the White House this morning."

"Well, I was," Rayburn said, "but I called the President and told him I had a friend who was in trouble, and I couldn't come."

Queen Victoria once shared her impressions of her two most famous prime ministers. Of William Gladstone, she said, "When I am with him, I feel I am with one of the most important leaders in the world." On the other hand, she confessed that when she was with Disraeli, he made her feel "as if *I am* one of the most important leaders of the world."

That reminds me of something my father once said. He was a school teacher up in the mountain districts. Over the years he served under a number of county school superintendents, two of whom (I'll call them Jones and Johnson) he once compared in this way. "When I went to Jones with a request, he could turn it down and make me feel good. But when I went to Johnson with a request, he would usually grant the request, but he always made me feel bad in the process."

That brings me to the third best thing I've ever heard about friendship. Andy Rooney once quipped: *Good old friends are worth keeping—whether you like them or not.*

Never ask yourself, "How can I find good friends?" Ask instead, "How can I be a better friend to someone else?" Imitate our Lord, who always takes the initiative in loving us. Find needs and meet them. Look for the lonely and love them. Remember birthdays. Make calls. Send notes. Be there in difficult times. Laugh with those who laugh, and weep with those who weep. Keep your friendships in good repair, and you'll be the richest person on the block. ৯৯

| 15 |

Solidarity

❦

No one played a larger role in the collapse of Communism in Eastern Europe than Karol Wojtyla of Krakow. During the Nazi occupation of Poland, Wojtyla had attended an underground Catholic seminary by dodging military patrols and taking secret classes in convents, churches, and homes. At length he graduated, donned clerical robes, and traveled to a small Polish village to serve as priest. Communists, meanwhile, were replacing Nazis as the oppressors of Eastern Europe, but with intrepidity, Wojtyla performed baptisms, heard confessions, offered Mass, foiled the Secret Police, and thwarted authorities.

The years passed, and by 1978, the village priest had advanced to become the first non-Italian pope in 456 years—John Paul II. On one of his first outings, the new pope heard someone in the crowd shout, "Don't forget the Church of Silence!" (that is, the church under

Communism). John Paul replied, "It's not a Church of Silence anymore, because it speaks with my voice."

John Paul soon returned in triumph to Warsaw where his plane landed over the protests of Soviet leader Leonid Brezhnev. Oceans of faces met him everywhere, weeping, praying, shouting. Communist leaders in Russia and Poland trembled as they listened to his words: "Dearest brothers and sisters! You must be strong with the strength that flows from faith! There is no need to be afraid. The frontiers must be opened."

Within a year, spontaneous strikes occurred throughout Poland, and in Gdansk, Lech Walesa stood atop an excavator and announced a strike in the shipyards. Back at the Vatican, John Paul watched, prayed, and spoke to a group of Polish pilgrims in St. Peter's Square. "All of us here in Rome are united with our compatriots in Poland," he said, signaling his blessings on the strikers. Within a week, the Communists made historic concessions, and on August 31, 1980, the Gdansk Accords were signed, permitting the first independent union in Eastern Europe. There was no mistaking the role of the Polish Pope, for Lech Walesa signed the papers using a brightly colored Vatican pen featuring a picture of John Paul II.

The Iron Curtain was crumbling. ❧

16

Watering the Weeds

❧❧❧

Some time ago as we were leaving for an extended vacation, I asked a friend to water and spray my rose bushes. When I returned, I couldn't see the rose bushes for the weeds.

"I don't know where those weeds came from," I told my wife. "They're taller than the rose bushes."

Come to find out, my friend saw the weeds starting to come up, and thinking they were bedding plants I'd planted among the roses, she sprayed and watered them, and doused them with a little extra fertilizer!

I later thought of the cultivation of my own life. Weeds—the bad habits—grow very quickly, and they can take over. The good habits, the disciplines of life, the roses, must be carefully cultivated.

Too many of us water the weeds.

The famous American psychologist William James said that by allowing separate acts to reoccur until they become habits _we are spinning our own fates, good or evil, and never to be undone._

Samuel Johnson put it this way: _The chains of habit are generally too small to be felt until they are too strong to be broken._

"Let us cast off the works of darkness," said the Apostle Paul in Romans 13, "and let us put on the armor of light. Let us walk properly, as in the day, not in revelry and drunkenness, not in lewdness and lust, not in strife and envy. But put on the Lord Jesus Christ, and make no provision for the flesh, to _fulfill its_ lusts." ❧

17

Fitting into My Loincloth

❧

Don't worry about doing something great," a missionary once told me. "Be great by doing what you can where God has placed you. It will pay off after awhile."

An old Moravian prayer says, "From the desire of being great, good Lord deliver us!"

When Charles Haddon Spurgeon, the 18th century Prince of Preachers, was eighteen years old, he was seeking God's will for his life. Feeling he needed more theological training, he made application to Regent's Park College, and an interview was set between the head of the college and young Spurgeon. The meeting was to be in Cambridge at the home of Mr. Macmillan, the publisher.

Spurgeon rose early that morning and had special prayer, seeking God's guidance in the matter, and then he proceeded to Mr. Macmillan's house. He rang the bell, and a servant showed him into the parlor. There he sat for two hours until at last his patience broke. He called for the servant and was horrified to discover that she had forgotten to announce his arrival, had not let anyone know he was there, had forgotten all about him.

Meanwhile the head of the college had sat waiting in an adjoining room until his patience, too, had been exhausted, and he had left Cambridge for London by train without the interview ever having taken place.

Spurgeon was deeply perturbed, and his first impulse was to run after the man, to chase him to London, to explain what had happened. But he took a long walk out in the country to calm down, and as he walked along, a verse of Scripture came to his mind so forcibly that he almost seemed to hear it audibly. He later said that it could not have been any clearer if Christ Himself had appeared to speak it aloud, so strong did this verse suddenly hit his mind. It was Jeremiah 45:5: *And do you seek great things for yourself? Do not seek them!*

The Lord seemed to be telling him not to worry about the misunderstanding and not to make extraordinary efforts to clear it up. As a result, Spurgeon never did make it to college, but it didn't matter. He became the most powerful and successful and fruitful minister in the history of Victorian England, and he later said that he "a thousand times thanked the Lord very heartily for the strange providence which forced his steps into another and far better path."

Missionary statesman J. Oswald Sanders once wrote about a time when he wanted a particular position in the Christian world very much. Having friends in positions of influence, he was about to see if some strings could be pulled to turn the job in his direction. He was toying with the idea of doing a little lobbying.

But while walking down the main street in Auckland, New Zealand one day, turning the matter over in his mind, he walked past His Majesty's Theatre and a verse of Scripture came to his mind with tremendous authority and powerful conviction: *And do you seek great things for yourself? Do not seek them!* (Jeremiah 45:5)

"The words came just as though it was God speaking. There were crowds all around me, and no one else heard the voice, but I heard it all right!" Sanders later said. "I believe that was a real turning point in my service to the Lord." As a result, he did not seek the position, but it later opened to him on its own in God's good timing.

As a young man, I had the opportunity of working for awhile with the Billy Graham Evangelistic Association. During one of Mr. Graham's crusades, I kept scheming to meet the great evangelist and to have my picture taken with him. At the same time, I was reading through the Gospel of John.

That's when I came to chapter 13.

In John 13, as Jesus began to wash the disciples' feet, He removed His garments. The use of the plural indicates that Jesus removed both His seamless robe and his tunic, which was a sort of long undershirt. That left Him in nothing but loincloth and sandals.

It wasn't necessary to strip so completely just to wash feet. The act of washing a guest's feet was a biblical custom which anyone could—and usually did—perform fully clothed. Why, then, did Jesus remove his garments?

The loincloth was the garb of an oriental servant, a slave. Our Lord was showing us that the Son of Man, who had laid aside the garments of heavenly glory to come to this earth, did so as one taking the form of a servant (Philippians 2:7).

And the Son of Man expects the same attitude in us as well.

I forgot about meeting Billy Graham and focused instead on fitting nicely into my loincloth.

"Many through wishing to be great have failed to be good," said Spurgeon.

Jesus put it this way: *Whoever desires to become great among you shall be your servant. And whoever of you desires to be first shall be slave of all. For even the Son of Man did not come to be served, but to serve, and to give His life a ransom for many.* (Mark 10:43–45) ॐ

18

Read It Some More

❧❦❧

R. A. Torrey (1856½1928), the great preacher and Bible teacher, was once approached by a Dr. Congdon, who complained that he could get nothing out of his Bible study. The Scripture seemed to be dry as dust.

"Please tell me how to study it so that it will mean something to me."

"Read it," replied Dr. Torrey.

"I do read it."

"Read it some more."

"How?"

Dr. Torrey suggested, "Take some book and read it twelve times a day for a month."

"What book could I read that many times a day, working as many hours as I do?"

"Try Second Peter," replied Torrey.

The man later said, "My wife and I read Second Peter

three or four times in the morning, two or three times at noon, and two or three times at dinner. Soon I was talking Second Peter to everyone one I met. It seemed as though the stars in the heavens were singing the story of Second Peter. I read Second Peter on my knees, marking passages. Teardrops mingled with the crayon colors, and I said to my wife, ''See how I have ruined this part of my Bible.''

"Yes," she said, "but as the pages have been getting black, your life has been getting white." 〰

19

Messiah

❧

He was a has-been, a fossil, a relic, an old fogy . . . but it hadn't always been so. As a child, George Frideric Handel had accompanied his father to the court of Duke Johann Adolf. Idly wandering into the chapel, the boy found the organ and started improvising, causing Duke Adolf to exclaim, "Who is this remarkable child?"

This "remarkable child" soon began composing operas, first in Italy, then in London. By his twenties he was the talk of England and the best paid composer on earth. He opened the Royal Academy of Music, and the next several years were intoxicating. Londoners fought for seats at his every performance, and his fame soared around the world.

But the glory passed. Audiences dwindled. His music became outdated. The Academy went bankrupt, and newer artists eclipsed the aging composer. One project after another failed, and Handel grew depressed. The stress brought on a case of palsy that crippled some of his fingers. "Handel's great days are over," wrote Frederick the Great, "his inspiration is exhausted."

Yet his troubles also matured him, softening his sharp tongue. His temper mellowed, and his music became more heartfelt. One morning Handel received by post a script from Charles Jennens. It was a word-for-word collection of various biblical texts about Christ. The opening words from Isaiah 40 moved Handel: *Comfort ye my people.* . . .

On August 22, 1741, he shut the door of his London home and started composing music for the words. Twenty-three days later, the world had *Messiah*. "Whether I was in the body or out of the my body when I wrote it, I know not," Handel later said, trying to describe the experience.

Messiah opened in London to enormous crowds on March 23, 1743. Handel led from his harpsichord, and King George II, who was present that night, surprised everyone by leaping to his feet during the *Hallelujah Chorus*. No one knows why. Some believe the king, being hard of hearing, thought it the national anthem. No matter—from that day audiences everywhere have stood in reverence during the stirring words: _Hallelujah! For He shall reign forever and ever._ ॐ

20

Contentment

❧❦❧

B ud Robinson, a well-known Holiness preacher of an earlier generation, was taken by friends to New York and shown around the city. That night in his prayers he said, "Lord, I thank You for letting me see all the sights of New York. And I thank You most of all that I didn't see a thing that I wanted!"

Contentment isn't a matter of having everything we want, but of not wanting everything we see. ❧

21

Some Snake Stories

❧❦❧

I'm not fond of snakes, and, knowing that, some missionary friends deliberately regaled me with their snake stories during my first mission trip to the Ivory Coast of West Africa.

"One night when I couldn't sleep," said one, "I slipped into the guest room and knelt in the darkness to pray. I felt something glide over my feet. Jumping up and turning on the light, I found I was sharing the room with a cobra."

"That's nothing," said another. "I walked into my tool shed recently and a cobra that had been nesting in the rafters fell on top of me."

Another told of preaching in a village church. "Every time I raised my hand in a gesture, I could see the audience pull back in alarm. When I'd lower my arm, they'd all exhale in unison. I thought I was making an impression on them by my sermon until one of them stood up and begged me to stop gesturing. "There's a cobra coiled in the beams right above the pulpit," he said. "Every time you lift your arm, we're afraid he's going to strike."

They killed the snake, then resumed the service.

It was one of the missionary women, however, whose story made me utterly paranoid for the remainder of my time in Africa. "Well," said Alice Smith, "my problem beats them all. We once had a cobra in the sewer system that kept slithering up through the toilets."

But nothing tops the snake story belonging to Moravian missionary Louis Daehne, who settled along the northern coast of South America, among the Arawak Indians in Dutch Guiana (Surinam). There he found enough danger for a dozen lifetimes.

Often Daehne was awakened at night by the roar of jaguars prowling around his hut for food. He was once attacked by poisonous black ants, each one an inch long and packed with venom, which stung him until he dropped to the ground senseless. On another occasion, his hut was surrounded by fifty bloodthirsty Indians wanting to kill him. Coming out to meet them, he began telling them of the Lord Jesus, and the headhunters were completely disarmed by the Gospel.

But perhaps his most harrowing experience involved a large snake that slithered into his hut and coiled on a shelf above his hammock. When Daehne unwittingly threw himself on his hammock to rest, the snake uncoiled and slithered over his head and face, biting him in the neck and injecting him with its venom.

Daehne gripped the writhing serpent, but in the scuffle it bit him several more times, fasting hard on his head and winding its cable-like body around his neck. The missionary struggled furiously, but the snake was a powerful one. Finally giving up, Daehne reached for a piece of chalk and wrote on the table by the hammock, "A serpent has killed me."

But just as he finished writing those words, Mark 16:18 flashed to his mind: "They will take up serpents . . . it will by no means hurt them." Summoning his last ounce of strength, Daehne gripped the snake again, wretched it loose, and flung it from the hut.

After recovering from the shock, Louis Daehne suffered no ill effects.

I'm not sure why God made snakes, or why Noah let them on his ark, but they surely serve some purpose, if only that of giving us a few exciting experiences and good stories. And that, after all, is worth a good deal. ✍

22

Seek Ye First

❦

J. Hudson Taylor, missionary pioneer to China and founder of the China Inland Mission (now Overseas Missionary Fellowship), left behind him generations of Taylors who would take up his torch. But perhaps none of his descendants ever faced a greater crisis than James and Alice Taylor who served the Lord during China in the 1930s. Their four children were trapped in boarding school in Chefoo when the Japanese invaded in 1937. Communication and transportation became impossible, with the only news in circulation being horror stories of Japanese atrocities.

Alice's imagination played havoc with her as she pictured her children being starved, raped, killed, or forced into battle. Her fears deepened upon learning that the school at Chefoo had been occupied by Japanese troops, the children being forced into a grim concentration camp.

Months stretched into years and the strain seemed unending. Her worst moment came upon hearing of the attack on Pearl Harbor. A bad situation for expatriated Americans became desperate.

"Oh, dear God," Alice whispered, kneeling by her bed, "my children, my children. . . ." Waves of anguish wracked her body, then paralyzing fear, then gulping sobs. "Dear God, are they even alive? . . . Please help my children. . . ."

Suddenly her mind traveled back to the words her old minister, Pa Ferguson, who once told her, "Alice, if you take care of the things that are dear to God, He will take care of the things that are dear to you." It was his personal translation of Matthew 6:33: *But seek first the kingdom of God and His righteousness, and all these things shall be added to you.*

A deep peace replaced her agony. Though she did not know whether her children were dead or alive, she realized that the war had not changed God's promise.

Earnestly committing her children to His keeping, she rose to do the work of God. Day after day, she took care of things dear to Him—teaching, comforting, treating the sick, reaching the Chinese with the Gospel. And the assurance stayed with her that God was taking care of those dear to her.

More years passed.

She later wrote: *I longed to hear some word, just to know. . . . And as I sat one September evening in our home during a faculty meeting, my mind wandered once more to the children. Again I pictured them as I had seen them last, waving goodbye. I heard their voices, faintly, calling excitedly. Then I heard their voices louder. Was I imagining this? No, their voices were real! And they came, bursting through the doorway. "Mommy, Daddy, we're home! We're home!" And they flew into our arms. Our hugs, our shouts filled the room. We couldn't let go of one another. It had been five and a half long, grueling years. Yet there they were—thin, but alive and whole, laughing and crying.*

Alice Taylor had taken care of the things important to God—and He had taken care of those important to her.* ঞ

---

*(For a fuller account along with the story of one particular boy, David Mitchell, who was interred with the Taylor children at Chefoo, see *A Boy's War* by David Mitchell [Singapore: Overseas Missionary Fellowship, 1988]. This story is adapted from pages 138–142.)

23

A Strong Tower

⋘⋙

Martin Niemöller was born on January 14, 1892, in Lippstadt, Westphalia. After serving as a German submarine commander during World War I, he studied theology in Münster and was ordained a minister of the church in Westphalia in 1924. He watched with growing concern the developing Nazi movement and the anti-Semitic rhetoric of Adolf Hitler.

In 1934, Hitler summoned Niemöller along with other German church leaders to his Berlin office to berate them for insufficiently supporting his programs. Niemöller explained that he was concerned only for the welfare of the church and of the German people. Hitler snapped, "You confine yourself to the church. I'll take care of the German people."

As the meeting was breaking up, Niemöller fired his final shot, "You said that 'I will take care of the German people.' But we too, as Christians and churchmen, have a responsibility toward the German people. That responsibility was entrusted to us by God, and neither you nor anyone in this world has the power to take it from us."

Hitler listened in stony silence, but that evening his Gestapo raided Niemöller's rectory, and a few days later a bomb exploded in his church. During the months and years following, he was closely watched by the secret police, and in June 1937, he preached these words to his church: "We have no more thought of using our own powers to escape the arm of the authorities than had the apostles of old. We must obey God rather than man." He was soon arrested and placed in solitary confinement.

Dr. Niemöller's trial began on February 7, 1938. That morning, a green-uniformed guard escorted the minister from his prison cell and through a series of underground passages toward the courtroom. Niemöller was overcome with terror and loneliness. What would become of him? Of his family? His church? What tortures awaited them all?

The guard's face was impassive, and he was as silent as stone. But as they exited a tunnel to ascend a final flight of stairs, Niemöller heard a slight whisper. At first he didn't know where it came from, for the voice was as soft as a sigh. Then he realized that the officer was breathing into his ear the words of Proverbs 18:10: *The name of the Lord is a strong tower; The righteous run to it and are safe.*

Niemöller's fear fell away, and the power of that verse sustained him through his trial and his years in Nazi concentration camps. ❧

24

Cedric

❧

By profession, I'm a communicator—a writer and public speaker. I'm supposed to be good at it, and I get paid for it. But in practice, I struggle to communicate with my kids just like you do. For example, one day as I drove my thirteen-year-old to piano practice, we managed to squeeze this conversation into the fifteen-minute trip:

"Hannah?"

"Huh?"

"How was your day?"

"Okay."

"Anything unusual happen? Any assembly programs? Any fights?"

"No, Dad. It was a normal day."

(Pause.) "Were all your friends at school today?"

"Yeah." (Pause.) "You sure ask a lot of questions."

"That's because I'm interested in the things that happened to you today."

"Well, nothing happened today."

(Pause.) "Any homework?"

"A little. But I can get it done before bedtime."

"Need any help?"

"Nope."

"I hope you have a good piano lesson."

"Thanks, Dad."

Later, when I pulled curbside, Hannah hopped in and said, "Dad, did I tell you about the dog with gas."

"The dog with what?"

"With gas."

"No, but I wish that truck would get out of my way."

"It was a boxer named Cedric."

"Hannah, I'm going to be late for my appointment, as sure as the world."

"Well, he was a beautiful dog, but you couldn't stay in the same room with him because . . ."

"Good grief! That light's gonna catch me."

". . . because every minute or two a terrible odor would fill the room. Sometimes he'd make a bad sound, and other times you just smelled it."

"I don't think I like this story, Hannah. Where did you hear it?"

"I read it last night in the James Herriot book of dog stories you gave me."

"Oh."

"Well, Cedric's owner called Dr. Herriot, but he couldn't help. She didn't want to put her dog to sleep, but no one could stand his exhaust."

"We're almost home; be ready to jump out."

"Cedric's owner finally decided to give him to a neighbor. Everyone wondered how the man could live with Cedric."

"I'm never going to make it to the office on time."

"Well, one day Dr. Herriot came to visit. As he walked into the room an odor rose from the dog. The doctor stuck his nose in a vase of flowers nearby, pretending to admire them. 'A friend gave those roses to me,' said the man. 'But I don't get the full benefit. I had an operation for adenoids when I was a kid, and something went wrong. I have no sense of smell.'"

At that, Hannah erupted into chortling. At the same moment, I pulled into our driveway and prepared to push her from the car. And then I realized . . . I realized that Hannah had just led me into her inner world. She had told me what had captured her attention at bedtime last night, what she'd been talking about with her friends that morning. She had told me the little story that had made her smile all day.

She had told me all that, and I had almost missed it.

I touched her arm as she started out the door. "His name was Cedric?" I asked.

She turned, our eyes met, we laughed, and for the first time that afternoon, we committed first-degree communication.

I learned a couple of things that night. First, if I expect my kids to tell me what I want to know, I need to listen to what they want to say. Second, I need to capitalize on key moments for communication, those spontaneous times when barriers are down and both parties are relaxed. ⤳

| 25 |

Foxe's Book of Martyrs

❧❧❧

According to the latest estimates, 150,000 people are martyred each year for the sake of Christ, and two million are actively persecuted. World Evangelical Fellowship reports that more people have died in circumstances related to their faith in the twentieth century than in all the twentieth century wars combined.

Unfortunately, persecution is nothing new. The apostles were whipped, Stephen was stoned, Paul was beheaded, and our Lord was crucified. The history of the church is written in blood, and those who know its history are most qualified to write its future.

That's why John Foxe, the great chronicler of persecution is so important. Christians of earlier eras kept a copy of his *Book of Martyrs* on the bookshelf beside their Bibles.

John Foxe, born in Lincolnshire, England, in 1516, was a brilliant young man who entered Oxford when he was only sixteen. News of Luther's Reformation was infiltrating university life in England, and young Foxe, intrigued, began pouring over the Scripture, trying to determine their true teaching. At length, he turned from Roman Catholicism to Protestantism, accepting the doctrine by justification by grace through faith alone.

His was a sensitive spirit, and often at night he would take long walks, weeping and pouring out his soul to the Lord in prayer. As a result of his Protestant "fanaticism" he was expelled from Oxford and, through the help of friends, became a private tutor in Stratford-on-Avon. Here he fell in love with Agnes Randall, and the two were married.

Their Protestant views caused them much trouble, for the pope's inquisitors were never far away. Through the help of family and friends, however, he remained secure and at liberty throughout the reigns of King Henry VIII and his son Edward VI, and into the reign of Queen Mary I.

But Mary was fiercely Catholic, and she waged a terrible crusade against the Protestants, forcing the Foxes (along with many others) to flee to the Continent. They traveled through Strasbourg, France, Germany, and on to Switzerland where they took up temporary residence.

It was while in Switzerland that John Foxe heard horrible news filtering in from England. Great Christian leaders such as Hugh Latimer, Nicholas Ridley, and Thomas Cramner, were being captured, tortured, and burned alive. It was a killing time, and scores of believers were perishing amid great pain and persecution.

It came sharply into Foxe's mind that someone should tell their stories. And he decided to do it himself, to compile a record of the persecution of God's people and give personal accounts of those who had suffered and died for Christ, especially during the inquisitions of Queen Mary.

Despite living on the edge of poverty, Foxe spent every spare moment on his project. He labored by day in Oporinus of Basel's printing shop to support his family, but by night he poured over his manuscript. He researched thoroughly, interviewed, and collected reports. His writing style was vivid, giving details, painting word pictures.

Finally the first version was ready, and in 1559, Foxe published his book on the Continent—732 pages in Latin. Returning to England under Protestant Elizabeth, he resumed pastoral work and translated his book into English. John Day published it in London in 1563 under the title *Acts and Monuments of These Latter and Perilous Days Touching Matters of the Church.*

But Foxe wasn't finished. He spent another four years traveling across England, interviewing witnesses, tracking down documents, finding letters. After long days of church ministry, he sat by flickering candlelight, continuing his writing. In 1570, a second edition appeared—two large volumes totaling 2,315 pages—then a third and a fourth.

Foxe's *Book of Martyrs* was one of the most important events in Elizabeth's reign, having an extraordinary impact on Britain. Copies appeared in every cathedral alongside the Bible. Vicars read from it during Sunday services. Francis Drake read it aloud on the western seas. It inspired the Puritans. It took the world by storm. Still today, four hundred years later, it is among Christianity's most treasured books.

Foxe's *Book of Martyrs* also took a toll on the author's personal health, and he never recovered. He died from weariness on April 18, 1587. Giving us his life's crowning achievement. ❧

26

The Christmas Truce

❦

This story has been told in a variety of ways, but this is the researched version that appeared in newspapers nationwide on December 25, 1994 from the Associated Press, dateline London. I found it in my hometown paper, *The Elizabethton Star:*

Eighty years ago, on the first Christmas Day of World War I, British and German troops put down their guns and celebrated peacefully together in the no-man's land between the trenches.

The war, briefly, came to a halt.

In some places, festivities began when German troops lit candles on Christmas trees on their parapets so the British sentries a few hundred yards away could see them.

Elsewhere, the British acted first, starting bonfires and letting off rockets.

Pvt. Oswald Tilley of the London Rifle Brigade wrote to his parents: "Just you think that while you were eating your turkey etc. I was out talking and shaking hands with the very men I had been trying to kill a few hours before! It was astounding."

Both armies had received lots of comforts from home and felt generous and well-disposed toward their enemies in the first winter of the war, before the vast battles of attrition began in 1915, eventually claiming ten million lives.

All along the line that Christmas Day, soldiers found their enemies were much like them and began asking why they should be trying to kill each other.

The generals were shocked. High Command diaries and statements express anxiety that if that sort of thing spread it could sap the troops' will to fight.

The soldiers in khaki and gray sang carols to each other, exchanged gifts of tobacco, jam, sausage, chocolate and liquor, traded names and addresses and played soccer between the shell holes and barbed wire. They even paid mutual trench visits.

This day is called "the most famous truce in military history" by British television producer Malcolm Brown and researcher Shirley Seaton in their book "Christmas Truce," published in 1984.

And His name will be called . . .
Prince of Peace
—Isaiah 9:6 ❧

27

What Happened to the Bounty

❦

The English ship *Bounty,* commanded by Lieutenant William Bligh, journeyed to the South Pacific in 1787 to collect plants of the breadfruit tree. Sailors signed on gladly, considering the voyage a trip to paradise. Having no second-in-command, Captain Bligh appointed his young friend Fletcher Christian to the post. The *Bounty* stayed in Tahiti six months, and the sailors, led by happy-go-lucky Fletcher Christian, enjoyed paradise to the full. When the time came for departure, some of the men wanted to stay behind with their island girls. Three men, trying to desert, were flogged. The mood on ship darkened, and on April 28, 1789, Fletcher Christian staged the most famous mutiny in history. Bligh and his supporters were set adrift in an overloaded lifeboat (which they miraculously navigated thirty-seven hundred miles to Timor).

The mutineers aboard the _Bounty_ immediately began quarreling about what to do next. Christian returned to Tahiti where he left some of the mutineers, kidnapped some women, took some slaves, and with the remaining crew traveled a thousand miles to uninhabited Pitcairn Island. There the little group quickly unraveled. They distilled whiskey from a native plant. Drunkenness and fighting marked their colony. Disease and murder eventually took the lives of all the men except for one, Alexander Smith, who found himself the only man on the island, surrounded by an assortment of women and children.

Then an amazing change occurred. Smith found the _Bounty_'s neglected Bible. As he read it, he took its message to heart, then began instructing the little community. He taught the colonists the Scriptures and helped them obey its instructions. The message of Christ so transformed their lives that twenty years later in 1808, when the _Topaz_ landed on the island, it found a happy society of Christians, living in prosperity and peace, free from crime, disease, murder—and mutiny. Years later, the Bible fell into the hands of a visiting whaler who brought it to America, but in 1950 it was returned to the island. It now resides on display in the church in Pitcairn as a monument to its transforming message. ❧

28

The Great Chicago Fire

On a warm autumn evening in 1871, D. L. Moody was preaching in Chicago's Farwell Hall from Matthew 27:22: *Pilate said to them, "What then shall I do with Jesus who is called Christ?"*

Our eternal destiny, Moody thundered, *depends on our answer to Pilate's question: "What shall I do with Jesus?"* At the conclusion of his sermon, Moody said: *I wish you would take this text home with you and turn it over in your minds during the week, and next Sabbath we will decide what to do with Jesus of Nazareth.*

But there was no next Sabbath. As soloist Ira Sankey closed the meeting singing, "Today the Savior Calls," his voice was suddenly drowned out by cries of alarm. The Great Chicago Fire had started and was sweeping toward the Hall. Gas mains were exploding and the streets were clogged with panicked, fleeing humanity.

The Great Chicago Fire started around 9 o'clock on Sunday evening, October 8, 1871, somewhere in or very near O'Leary's barn. Whipped along by gusting winds, it spread quickly into and through the downtown areas, consuming everything in sight. Some observers later said that the ground itself seemed to burn, which is quite possible since the streets, sidewalks, and bridges were all made of wood. Even the river seemed aflame, for several vessels caught fire and the grease along the water's surface ignited.

Not until the following Tuesday morning did firefighters, helped by rain, manage to bring the fire under control. By Wednesday Chicago was a smoking, steaming, smoldering ruin. Gone were eighteen thousand buildings. One hundred thousand people were homeless.

Among them were the Moodys.

During that Sunday night, flames had leaped over the Chicago River and torched Moody's own street. In the ensuing bedlam, a neighbor took the Moody children in his crowded carriage and sought a northbound route of escape. Mr. and Mrs. Moody hastily threw some valuables into a box and prepared to follow.

Mrs. Moody was intent on saving one particular item—an oil portrait of her husband which the artist Healey had personally presented to her following Moody's first trip to Europe. Moody himself would have nothing to do with it, afraid someone would see him fleeing through the chaos clinging to a portrait of himself. His wife, however, prevailed, knocking the picture from its heavy gold frame and carrying it out herself.

In the Great Chicago Fire, Moody lost his home, his church, and much of the financial backing for his work. But he was most haunted by the lost opportunity of winning to Christ those to whom he had preached on that terrible evening.

Twenty-two years later on the anniversary of the fire, Moody again spoke in Chicago from Matthew 27:22, saying: *What a mistake! I remember Mr. Sankey's singing, and how his voice rang: "Today the Savior calls, for refuge fly! The storm of justice falls, and death is nigh!"*

I have never seen that congregation since. I have hard work keeping back the tears today. Twenty-two years have passed away, and I have not seen that congregation since, and I never will meet those people again until I meet them in another world. But I want to tell you of one lesson I learned that night, which I have never forgotten, and that is, when I preach, to press Christ upon the people then and there, and try to bring them to a decision on the spot.

You will notice that Pilate was just in the condition of my audience that night, just the condition that you are in today—he had to decide then and there what to do with Jesus. The thing was sprung on him suddenly.

I have asked God many times to forgive me for telling people that night to take a week to think it over. I have never dared to give an audience a week to think of their salvation since. ॐ

29

What a Day!

❧

Deeply shaken by the Great Chicago Fire of 1871 that destroyed his home and his life's work, Dwight L. Moody quickly left for New York, seeking funds for re-building his church and ministry. He also hoped to solicit money for the thousands of Chicagoians left homeless by the disaster.

But his heart was not in the work of begging, and as he later said, "I could not appeal. I was crying all the time that God would fill me with His Spirit."

In New York, Moody was walking down Wall Street when he had a spiritual experience so powerful that he seldom referred to it afterward.

Well, one day, in the city of New York—ah, what a day!— I cannot describe it. I seldom refer to it, it is almost too sacred an experience to name—Paul had an experience of which he never spoke for fourteen years—I can only say that God revealed Himself to me, and I had such an experience of His love that I had to ask Him to stay His hand. I went to preaching again. The sermons were not different; I did not present any new truths; and yet hundreds were converted. I would not now be placed back where I was before that blessed experience if you should give me all the world; it would be as the small dust of the balance.

From that day, whenever, wherever Moody preached, multitudes listened and hundreds were saved. His fame soared, and D. L. Moody spent the rest his life traveling the globe as the most famous and effective evangelist for Christ in the nineteenth century. ❧

30

Dying to Live

❧❦❧

Galatians 2:20 tells us the Christian lives a relinquished life: *I have been crucified with Christ.*

What does that mean? Among other things it means that followers of Christ have once upon a time come to the old rugged cross and have gazed upon the dying form of one who suffered there. We see His hands nailed fast to the wood. We see the spike in His ankles. We see the blood flowing in streaks down His body, and, deeply moved, we turn aside from the kind of life we once lived to take our stand beneath the cross of Jesus. We die to our old selves, we die to our sin, we die to the world, the flesh, and the devil, and we identify with the cross of Christ.

When James Calvert went out as a missionary to the cannibals of the Fiji Islands, the captain of the ship sought to dissuade him. "You will lose your life and the lives of those with you if you go among such savages," he cried.

Calvert only replied, "We died before we came here."

Dietrich Bonhoeffer, the German Christian who died in Nazi hands, once said, "When God calls a man, he bids him come and die."

Someone once asked the German Christian George Müeller, the secret of his victorious Christian life. He replied: *There came a day when George Müeller died, utterly died! No longer did his own desires, preferences, and tastes come first. He knew that from then on Christ must be all in all.*

My pastor during my college years in Columbia, South Carolina, was Dr. H. Edwin Young, who taught me much about preaching and pastoring. One day in his office he asked me if I knew the secret of Christian victory. He said, "You have to put 220 volts to yourself every day—Galatians 2:20. *I have been crucified with Christ.*"

Someone once saw this sign in the window of a dry-cleaning and dying business: *We dye to live, we live to dye;*

the more we dye, the more we live; and the more we live, the more we dye.

That's the slogan for the Christian. ও

31

Not Ready for Prime Time

❧

We've never been a particularly athletic family, but for awhile when my youngest daughter Grace was playing softball we became baseball fans. One day, wanting to do something special with her, I suggested an out-of-town trip to a major league game. I made the hotel reservations, rented the car, and we took off.

As we approached the stadium on game day, I noticed hundreds of colorful signs hanging from overpasses, attached to buildings, being sold or given away on the sidewalks. They were blaring out the words: "Neon Deion!"

"What's Neon Deion?" I asked.

"It's not a *What*. It's a *Who*," said Grace, "Deion Sanders. Plays center field. He's a little cocky, but he's my favorite player. He's *everyone's* favorite player!" And she proceeded to tell me everything she knew about this remarkable young man who excelled at both professional baseball and major league football.

When we entered the stadium, the first thing we saw was Neon Deion, warming up in the outfield. As I watched him, certain feelings swept through my mind.

Unknown to me at the time, Deion was having a totally different set of thoughts.

I was thinking to myself: "What would it feel like to race onto the field wearing a major league uniform, being cheered by thousands?"

Deion later wrote about that period of his life: _I was in a bad situation. I was on the brink of having the best year of my professional baseball career, but my stepfather had just passed away, my wife was divorcing me, and it was all over the newspapers that my family life was coming apart. . . . I began to think that it was over for me and, without realizing how bad off I was, I became suicidal._

In the stands that day, I thought: "They call him 'Mr. Millionaire Athlete,' and 'Prime Time Sanders.' He's on top of the world."

Deion later wrote: *I was running on empty, but I had to keep acting like I was the life of the party. Everybody depended on me for that. I was supposed to be the catalyst of the team. I was supposed to keep my energy and my attitude together . . . but I was barely holding on.*

As I watched Deion bound across home plate, I felt tiny pangs of envy, the kind guys feel. "What would it be like to be in his shoes?" I wondered.

The pain was horrible. Inconceivable. Anyone who has never had that experience can't begin to imagine what it was like to be in my shoes at that time. It was just crushing pain.

When the game ended, Grace and I rushed to the edge of the field, hoping to get a glimpse of Deion as he trotted off to the dressing room after the team's decisive victory. With a wave to the crowd, he ducked into the tunnel and disappeared.

I thought about the lifestyles of the rich and famous, but what was going on in Deion's mind?

I remember sitting on the bench one day and emptying a whole bottle of Tylenol 3 capsules into my mouth right in front of the whole team, and the players acted as if they didn't even see it. I was just crying out for someone to talk to me, to ask me about my situation, to care that I was dying inside, but who could have imagined that I was in so much pain. . . . I was hurting. I had plenty of money and everything else a man could want, but I was desperately empty inside. . . .

Grace and I went home with our memories and souvenirs, but I was surprised to read shortly afterward that Deion had tried to kill himself by barreling his custom-made sports car off the side of a cliff. I begin wondering if my twinges of jealousy were justified.

Then things changed for Deion Sanders, for some friends began sharing with him the message of Jesus Christ. One morning in the wee hours, opening his Bible to Romans 10:9–10, Deion read forty-three words that changed his life: "If you confess with your mouth the Lord Jesus and believe in your heart that God has raised Him from the dead, you will be saved. For with the heart one believes unto righteousness, and with the mouth confession is made unto salvation."

The words hit me like a ton of bricks. I knew they were meant for me, and at that precise moment I was delivered. I put my trust in Jesus and asked Him into my life. And as soon as I realized what I had done I was so excited I had to tell somebody, so I got on the phone and called my attorney and said, "Eugene, I did it!"

"What, Deion? What did you do?"

"I got saved."*

Jack Higgins, the renowned author of *The Eagle Has Landed,* once said that the one thing he knows now at this high point in his career that he wished he had known as a small boy is this: "When you get to the top, there's nothing there."

Looking back on that summer's day in Atlanta, I'm a little embarrassed for being even mildly jealous, for envy is a vice grounded in ignorance. "Most people are motivated to success by their envy of their neighbors," said King Solomon. "But this, too, is meaningless, like chasing the wind" (Ecclesiastes 4:4, NLT).

How much better to pray for those whom we envy than to covet the lifestyles of those desperately needing our prayers. ❧

---

*The Deion Sanders quotes are taken from Sanders, Deion. *Deion Sanders: Power, Money, & Sex—How Success Almost Ruined My Life.* (Nashville: Word Publishing, 1998).

32

Traveling to Calvary

∽§§∾

Dr. Eric Frykenberg, veteran missionary to India, was a great storyteller, and he could vividly describe scenes and events from his fifty-plus years in Asia. One day someone asked him, "Dr. Frykenberg, what is the most difficult problem you ever faced?"

Without hesitation, he answered, "It was when my heart would grow cold before God. When that happened, I knew I was too busy. I also knew it was time to get away. So I would take my Bible and go off to the hills alone. I'd open my Bible to Matthew 27, the story of the Crucifixion, and I would wrap my arms around the cross."

"And then," Frykenberg said, "I'd be ready to go back to work."

I once read of a man in Dundee, Scotland, who was confined to bed for forty years, having broken his neck in a fall at age fifteen. But his spirit remained unbroken, and his cheer and courage so inspired people that he enjoyed a constant stream of guests. One day a visitor asked him, "Doesn't Satan ever tempt you to doubt God?"

"Oh, yes," replied the man. "He does try to tempt me. I lie here and see my old schoolmates driving along in their carriages and Satan whispers, 'If God is so good, why does He keep you here all these years? Why did he permit your neck to be broken?'"

"What do you do when Satan whispers those things?" asked the guest.

"Ah," replied the invalid, "I take him to Calvary, show him Christ, and point to those deep wounds, and say, 'You see, he *does* love me.' And Satan has no answer to that. He flees every time." ॐ

33

The Word of a Gentleman

❦

As David Livingstone, the great missionary and explorer, journeyed down the Zambezi River, searching for the ultimate entrance into Central Africa from the Eastern Coast, he was wide-eyed. The country teemed with elephants, buffalo, and all kinds of wildlife. A thousand dangers encompassed him, from snakes to fevers to savages.

But even worse dangers threatened him as he left charted areas and pressed on toward unexplored regions filled with hostile tribes. His guides were nervous, nerves taut, motions quick. Reports filtered in of warriors and headhunters massing against them, ready to massacre his whole party.

At a critical juncture, when his guides were near revolt and his own fears were assailing him, Livingstone pulled his Bible from his baggage, opened it, and ran his finger again across his favorite passage, Matthew 28:20.

All authority has been given to Me in heaven and on earth.
Go therefore and make disciples of all the nations. . . .
I am with you always, even to the end of the age.

Living's courage revived like the rising sun, and in his journal that evening, January 14, 1856, he wrote: *Felt much turmoil of spirit in prospect of having all my plans for the welfare of this great region and this teeming population knocked on the head. But I read that Jesus said, "Lo, I am with you always, even unto the end of the world." It is the word of a gentleman of the most strict and sacred honor, so there's an end of it! I feel quite calm now, thank God!*

The next morning, he pressed on. *Nothing earthly shall make me give up my work in despair. I encourage myself in the Lord my God, and go forward.*

Later, having returned to Scotland and England on furlough, Livingstone was considered a national hero. When Glasgow University arranged a well-publicized ceremony honoring him, Livingstone spoke freely of his determination to soon return to Africa: *But I return without misgiving and with great gladness. For would you like me to tell you what supported me through all the years of exile among people whose language I could not understand, and whose attitude toward me was often hostile? It was this: "Lo, I am with you always, even unto the end of the world." On those words I staked everything, and they never failed.* ❧

34

Providence

❦

William and Marion Veitch, a godly Presbyterian couple, lived with their children in a peaceful home in Scotland in the 17th century. William was a preacher, but in those days the Presbyterian faith was outlawed, and he lived in fear that sooner or later he would be arrested. It happened one night in 1680. Royal Scottish soldiers burst in and dragged William foff to prison.

It was all orchestrated by a man named Thomas Bell, a vicar in the established church who drank and used profanity and harbored a burning hatred for the Veitchs.

William was taken to Morpeth Prison, leaving Marion at home profoundly troubled. Pouring out her soul to the Lord in prayer, she opened her Bible and drew strength from certain verses, such as "He does all things well," and "Trust in the Lord, and fear not what man can do." Then as soon as she could arrange it, she set off to visit her

husband, for it appeared he would be removed to Edinburgh and executed.

Marion's journey took place on a bitterly cold January
day. The snow was blinding, and she had to fight the
weather on horseback. Night fell, and she trudged on,
finally arriving at the prison, half-frozen, around midnight.

The guards wouldn't let her see William until morning, so Marion sat by the fire and waited. When morning
broke, she was allowed to see her husband for only a
moment, and only in the presence of guards. Then she
was torn away, expecting never to see him again.

Marion went to a friend's house, wept her fill, and
opened her Bible. The words of Isaiah 8:12–13 spoke
powerfully to her: . . . *Nor be afraid of their threats, nor be
troubled. The Lord of hosts, Him you shall hallow. Let Him be
your fear, And let Him be your dread*. She rested herself in
the Lord and cast her burden on Him.

Meanwhile their archenemy, Vicar Thomas Bell,
gloated to friends, "Now Veitch will be hanged tomorrow
as he deserves."

That evening Thomas Bell called on a friend and the
two lingered over the alcohol until about 10 P.M. when
he said he must be going. The night was dark and cold,
the river was icy and swollen, and his host urged him to

wait till morning. But Bell had work to do and victims to prosecute. He rode away warmed by alcohol, but he never reached home. Two days later his dead body was found standing up to his arms in one solid block of ice in the river.

William was soon freed, and the restored couple worked side-by-side until William's death forty years later.

The history of the church and the story of our lives are liberally sprinkled with incidents like this—God's overruling, undergirding sovereignty, God's protection, God's provision, and His answers to prayer.

In the unfolding of His providence, burdens become blessings, tears lead to triumph, and the redemptive grace of God overcomes the undercurrents of life in the experiences of His children. For them . . .

> *Ill that God blesses is our good,*
> *And unblest good is ill,*
> *And all is right that seems most wrong*
> *If it be His sweet will.*

This is Romans 8:28, lived out in daily experience: *. . . All things work together for good to those who love God, to* those who are called according to His purpose. Understanding the Sovereignty of God is one of the most liberating experiences a Christian can ever have.

John Calvin once said, _When the light of divine providence has once shone upon a godly man, he is then relieved and set free not only from the extreme anxiety and fear that were pressing him before, but from every care. . . . Ignorance of providence is the ultimate misery; the highest blessedness lies in knowing it. . . . [It gives] incredible freedom from worry about the future._

No wonder Charles Spurgeon once quipped, _We believe in the providence of God, but we do not believe half enough in it._ ৶

35

Bearing Fruit

❦

On May 8, 1984, Benjamin M. Weir, veteran Presby-terian missionary to Lebanon, was kidnapped at gunpoint by Shiite Muslims in Beirut. During his sixteen-month imprisonment, he was constantly threatened with death. On his first night in captivity, one of his abductors came to him, telling him to face the wall, which he did. "Now take your blindfold off and put this on." The man handed Benjamin a pair of ski goggles with the eye holes covered with thick plastic tape. They totally blocked out the light. In Weir's mind, the sun had set. He later wrote:

In the twilight there came to mind the hymn, "Abide with me / fast falls the eventide." I felt vulnerable, helpless, lonely. I felt tears in my eyes. Then I remembered the promise of Jesus, "If you abide in me and my words abide in you, ask what you will and it shall be done unto you."

"Lord, I remember Your promise, and I think it applies to

me, too. I've done nothing to deserve it but receive it as a free gift. I need You. I need Your assurance and guidance to be faithful to You in this situation. Teach me what I need to learn. Deliver me from this place and this captivity if it is Your will. If it is not Your will to set me free, help me to accept whatever is involved. Show me Your gifts, and enable me to recognize them as coming from You. Praise be to You."

For the next sixteen months, Benjamin Weir's hope and joy was found in the fact that he was not simply abiding in captivity. He was abiding in Christ, and thus able to "bear much fruit."*

How often this old hymn comes to comfort us with its Scripture-inspired words:

> *Abide with me! Fast falls the eventide.*
> *The darkness deepens; Lord, with me abide!*
> *When other helpers fail and comforts flee,*
> *Help of the helpless, oh, abide with me!* ஜ

_____

*Adapted from Benjamin M. Weir with Dennis Benson, "Tough Faith," *Leadership Journal,* Winter 1989, 55. Excerpted from the book, *Hostage Bound, Hostage Free.*

36

What Happened to the Dog

❦

One day as missionary Dick Hillis preached in a Chinese village, his sermon was suddenly interrupted by a piercing cry. Everyone rushed toward the scream, and Dick's coworker, Mr. Kong, whispered that an evil spirit had seized a man.

"That is heathen superstition," said Dick, who had not previously encountered demon possession. Just then a woman frantically pushed through the crowd toward them. "I beg you help me!" she cried. "An evil spirit has again possessed the father of my children and is trying to kill him."

The two men followed her to her small house nearby. As Mr. Kong entered the room, he had to step over a filthy old dog lying in the doorway. Inside was the frenzied madman, and the room was charged with a sense of evil.

"An evil spirit has possessed Farmer Ho," Kong told

the onlookers. "Our God, the 'Nothing-He-Cannot-Do One' is more powerful than any spirit, and He can deliver this man. First, you must promise you will burn your idols and trust in Jesus, son of the Supreme Emperor."

The people nodded. Kong asked Dick to begin singing the hymn "There is Power in the Blood." Still unsure of what was unfolding, Dick began to hesitantly sing, "Would you be free from your burden of sin . . ."

"Now," continued Kong, "in the name of Jesus we will command the evil spirit to leave this man." Kong began praying fervently, and as he did so the old dog in the doorway suddenly vaulted into the air, screeching, yelping, whirling in circles snapping wildly at his tail.

Kong continued praying, and the dog abruptly dropped over dead.

Instantly Dick remembered Luke 8, the demons of the Gadarenes who invisibly flew into the herd of swine. As Kong finished praying, Farmer Ho seemed quiet and relaxed, and soon he was strong enough to burn his idols. At his baptism shortly afterward, he testified, "I was possessed by an evil spirit who boasted he had already killed five people and was going to kill me. But God sent Mr. Kong at just the right moment, and in Jesus I am free."

We are more surrounded than we know by the foul spirits of hell, more protected than we know by the strong grace of Christ, and the battle is often closer than we realize. &

37

How Not *to Parent*

❦

Olympic superstar Greg Louganis's mom encouraged him in his gymnastics and diving. Her only comment before a performance was, "Have fun!" But his father, a severe and distant man, virtually ignored him until he showed signs of greatness. Then he pushed him relentlessly, and Greg found himself becoming the rope in a tug-of-war between his parents.

One day eleven-year-old Greg couldn't make himself try a new and dangerous dive. He was scared and mentally unprepared, and it was cold. He just stood on the board, frozen. Finally his coach said, "Let's try tomorrow."

Greg's father, watching the whole thing, smoldered. Once home he snapped, "Get your suit on." The boy protested, but reluctantly suited up. The dad whipped off his belt and repeatedly lashed him, but Greg held back tears, refusing to give his father the satisfaction of seeing him cry. A few minutes later, shivering on the edge of the diving board, he jumped. Again and again he threw himself into the unheated pool, purposely doing it wrong, hitting the water flat, replacing pain with pain.

Shortly afterward, Greg tried to kill himself. And despite eventually becoming one of America's most famous divers, Louganis has lived a sad and painful life, tormented by doubt and abuse, a life-threatening diagnosis, "a lonely boy." As he puts it he is, "a man who had a world of opportunities yet lost his way when those opportunities ended."

Louganis's story illustrates one of the most difficult balances of parenting. How do we encourage our children to do their best without twisting their arms or banging their heads? How can we prompt them to excellence without provoking them to wrath? When should we say, "Have fun?" And when should we push them to "Go for the gold!"

Perhaps no concept in modern times has tyrannized parents like that of the average child. We desperately long for our children to be above average, to be better looking, to make better grades and to have more skills than the next kid. We feel pangs of worry if another couple's baby talks or walks or is potty trained before ours. We study our children's achievement tests to make sure the score is to the right of the median.

Ephesians 6:4 gives us the answer: *And you, fathers, do not provoke your children to wrath, but bring them up in the training and admonition of the Lord.*

The word *provoke* is a Greek word meaning to frustrate, to anger. It means "do not exasperate your children or instill within them an angry disposition." This doesn't mean that our children will never become angry at our decisions. It means we shouldn't be overly strict, angry, overprotective, lax, lenient, absent, or critical so as to make our children embittered in their hearts.

This term *bring them up* is a Greek word—*ektrepho*—found only twice in the Bible, here and in Ephesians 5:29: *After all, no one hated his own body, but he feeds it and cares for it, just as Christ does the church* (NIV).

The root word *trepho* means to provide nourishment. This is the word Jesus used when he told us to consider how the Heavenly Father feeds the birds of the air. It's also the word used in Acts 12:20 when the people of Tyre and Sidon approached King Herod to talk about their food supply. This is also the word used in Luke 4, when it says that Jesus returned to the town of Nazareth where he had been brought up.

The idea is that parents are to provide the nourishment children need for growth. Not just the physical nourishment of food on the table, but the emotional and spiritual and mental nourishment children need.

Finally, the word admonition—*nouthesia*—comes from the word *nous,* meaning, *mind;* and *tithami,* meaning, *to deposit.* So literally it means *to deposit in the mind.* It is often translated *to warn.* It suggests that parents are responsible for depositing the truths of God's Word into the minds and hearts of their children.

None of us are perfect parents, but those who know the Lord Jesus Christ, who love Him and are filled with His Spirit have the ability to get off the ground, to soar into the sky, to reach heaven and funnel some of God's grace down for our children. We must find the time to listen and to love and, with the Lord's help, to bring up our children in the training and in the instruction of the Lord. ৪৺

38

A Brother's Prayers

❧

Jimmy Modha, who was raised in a devout Hindu home in Leicester, England, enraged his family by coming to Christ and converting to Christianity. He told them his sins had been forgiven because he had found God.

"Which god?" shouted his father.

"It's Jesus Christ," replied Jimmy. "Actually He came and found me. He died on the cross for my sins; I am a Christian."

Jimmy's mother fainted, his father threw him out of the house, and his brother Jay prayed for the gods to kill him. "We would mourn his death," said Jay, "but at least our family would not be dishonored."

Jay, a brilliant student working on his Ph.D. in parasitology at the London School of Hygiene and Tropical Medicine at the University of London, disowned his brother and refused to talk to him. Jimmy was deeply hurt, but in parting, he said, "Jay, if you are ever desperate and no one is there to help you, remember Jesus loves you and His hand is on your life. Call to Him and He will save you."

Jay was furious, but Jimmy began praying earnestly for him.

Shortly Jay began having disturbing dreams. "It was as if I was awake in my bed at three in the morning when suddenly a blinding light broke through the roof and ceiling of my bedroom. In that light I could see a cloud descending from heaven, bearing three awesome, fiery men-like creatures. The first blew a trumpet so loud that I was sure the whole world could hear its thunderous sound. I knew whatever was coming was universal in consequence. The second creature cried out, 'Prepare ye, for the Lord is coming to reap the harvest!' Then the third swung a scythe over the earth and cried, 'Now is the earth ready for harvest!'

"I tried to wake up from the dream because I felt I was going to have a heart attack from sheer fright. But I could not. Then, in the middle of the cloud, I noticed a Person who looked completely different. The brilliant light was coming from Him. His face shone so radiantly that no features were clear except for eyes that looked like blazing flames of fire. A robe went from His neck to His feet, which were like white-hot metal. He was dreadful in His beauty and terrible in His splendor.

"As He descended, He looked at me. I was completely undone, absolutely terrified. I could not bear to look at Him any longer, so I turned my head. To my amazement, there beside me was my brother Jimmy, who was not scared at all. In fact, his face was joyous, and he was reaching out as if to embrace the figure.

"When I gained the courage to look at Him again, He addressed me saying, 'Jay, what are you going to do when this happens?' Then everything vanished, and I woke up."

It took Jay an hour to calm down, and he prayed for understanding.

A few days later, Jimmy called and, hearing of Jay's dream, said, "Jay, what you saw was the Second Coming of Christ. Can I send you a Bible so you can read about it?" Jay hung up. But more dreams disturbed his sleep, and one night he awoke horrified to find he had been dreaming of praying to Jesus. In time, Jay received his doctorate and was awarded a prestigious research fellowship in Japan. But in Japan, his mental state deteriorated and one night, standing on his balcony, he nearly leaped to his death. But at the last minute, he pushed himself away from the railing, vowing to find out if Jesus was, in fact, the living and true God. For two years, God pursued him and every waking moment Jay felt the wrath of God hovering over him. At length, he dug from a cupboard a dust-covered old Bible and began to read in the Gospels. When he got to the Lord's words from the cross, "Father, forgive them, for they don't know what they do," Jay realized that he was a sinner for whom Christ had died. He prayed for forgiveness and the burden of his guilt lifted.

Jay grew quickly and, moving to Glasgow, joined a church and in time began teaching and preaching. Concluding that God was calling him into the ministry, he enrolled in Reformed Theological Seminary to prepare to preach the Gospel he had once so fervently resisted.

In seeking to win our loved ones to Christ, we can do what we can do, but we can't do what only God can do. Our job is to pray, love, witness, and model Christ. God's part is to convict, convert, and transform from within. Don't grow discouraged if He takes a while to reach your brother, son, or friend. Give Him time, but don't stop praying; for "the effective, fervent prayer of a righteous man avails much" (James 5:16). ❧

39

Therefore We Must Go Forward

❧❧

Wﬁlliam Carey, the "Father of Modern Missions," wanted to translate the Bible into as many Indian languages as possible. He established a large printshop at his mission headquarters in Serampore, India where translation work was continually being done. Carey spent hours each day translating Scripture.

He was away from Serampore on March 11, 1832, when disaster struck. His associate, William Ward, was working late. Suddenly Ward's throat tightened and he smelled smoke. He leaped up to discover clouds belching from the printing room. He screamed for help, and workers passed water from the nearby river until 2 A.M., but everything was destroyed.

The next day, fellow missionary Joshua Marshman

traveled to Calcutta and entered the classroom where William was teaching. "I can think of no easy way to break the news," he said. "The printshop burned to the ground last night."

Carey was stunned. Gone were his massive polyglot dictionary, two grammar books, and whole versions of the Bible. Gone were sets of type for fourteen eastern languages, twelve hundred reams of paper, fifty-five thousand printed sheets, and thirty pages of his Bengal dictionary. Gone was his complete library.

"The work of years—gone in a moment," he whispered.

He took little time to mourn. "The loss is heavy," he wrote, "but as traveling a road the second time is usually done with greater ease and certainty than the first time, so I trust the work will lose nothing of real value. We are not discouraged, indeed the work is already begun again in every language. We are cast down but not in despair."

When news of the fire reached England, it catapulted Carey to instant fame. Thousands of pounds were raised for the work, and volunteers offered to come help. The enterprise was rebuilt and enlarged. By 1832, complete Bibles, New Testaments, or separate books of Scripture had issued from the printing press in forty-four languages and dialects.

The secret of Carey's success is found in his resiliency. "There are grave difficulties on every hand," he once wrote, "and more are looming ahead. Therefore we must go forward." ❧

40

More Courage Among the Flames

❧❧❧

In December 1914, a great, sweeping fire destroyed Thomas Edison's laboratories in West Orange, New Jersey, wiping out two million dollars' worth of equipment and the record of much of his life's work.

Edison's son Charles ran about frantically trying to find his father. Finally he came upon him, standing near the fire, his face ruddy in the glow, his white hair blown by the winter winds. "My heart ached for him," Charles Edison said. "He was no longer young, and everything was being destroyed. He spotted me. 'Where's your mother?' he shouted. 'Find her. Bring her here. She'll never see anything like this again as long as she lives.'"

The next morning, walking about the charred embers of so many of his hopes and dreams, the sixty-seven-year-old Edison said, "There is great value in disaster. All our mistakes are burned up. Thank God we can start anew."*

Jeremiah, looking at the smoldering ruins of Jerusalem, said the same thing in Lamentations 2:22–24:

> Through the LORD's mercies we are not consumed,
> Because His compassions fail not.
> They are new every morning;
> Great is Your faithfulness.
> "The LORD is my portion," says my soul,
> "Therefore I hope in Him!" ﺨﻤ

_____

*Adapted from Alan Loy McGinnis in *The Power of Optimism* (New York: Harper & Row, 1990). 15–16.

41

Down to His Underwear

❦

How literally should we interpret verses like Luke 6:30, which says, *Give to everyone who asks of you. And from him who takes away your goods do not ask them back?*

One man determined to obey this command to the letter. He was Henry Richards, missionary to Africa with the Livingstone Inland Mission (now part of World Team). After arriving in Africa, he began his ministry in the village of Banza Mateke by translating the Gospel of Luke into the local tribal language. He would translate a handful of verses each day, and regularly preach to the tribe from the verses he had translated.

It all went well until he came to Luke 6:30. How could he read this verse to the people, he wondered, and how could he possibly explain it? *Give to everyone who asks of you. And from him who takes away your goods do not ask them back.*

The village was full of beggars, and it was common-place for the curious villagers to ask him for everything he possessed. He feared that if he actually gave his sparse missionary possessions to everyone who asked for them, he would be soon reduced to his underwear.

Richards went back to chapter one and started preaching through Luke again, to reinforce the Gospel message—and to give himself more time to ponder the problem posed by Luke 6:30. In time, he grew convinced that it meant exactly what it said, so when he came to it he read it plainly.

Immediately the villagers in Banza Mateke began asking him for his belongings. He began distributing his goods as requested, and was soon reduced to near-underwear status. But to Richards' surprise, the people suddenly began returning his things, and before long every single item was back in its place. "What did it mean?" wondered the missionary.

Richards later learned that as the villagers had talked among themselves, they concluded that such an unselfish man must indeed be God's man, and that his message must be God's message, for God "so loved that he gave . . ."

As a result of that incident, the people of Banza

Mateke opened their hearts to Henry Richards and to his message, and a period of widespread revival and awakening transformed the village.

"He who sows sparingly will also reap sparingly, and he who sows bountifully will also reap bountifully. So let each one give as he purposes in his heart, not grudgingly or of necessity; for God loves a cheerful giver. And God is able to make all grace abound toward you, that you, always having all sufficiency in all things, may have an abundance for every good work" (2 Corinthians 9:6–8). ॐ

42

Eleanor Porter's Little Girl

❦

Proverbs 15:30 says: *The light of the eyes rejoices the heart, And a good report makes the bones healthy.*

In other words, when you look at other human beings with cheerfulness, it brings joy and life to their own spirits. They are lifted up and encouraged. The Amplified Bible translates this verse: *The light of the eyes of him whose heart is joyful rejoices the heart of others;* and the Good News Bible simply says, *Smiling faces make you happy.*

This is the real meaning behind the famous children's book *Pollyanna,* written by Eleanor Porter in 1913.

Eleanor was born in Littleton, New Hampshire, in 1828 and studied at the New England Conservatory of Music in Boston, wanting to be a singer. She developed a following in the Boston area and poured herself into Christian music and singing in church choirs. But by the early

1900s her writing instincts had taken over, and several of her short stories began appearing in popular magazines.

Her first novel was published in 1907, and her most famous work, *Pollyanna,* appeared in 1913. It sold over a million volumes and spawned a whole line of books. It was dramatized in 1916 and later made into a movie with Mary Pickford. It was later remade by Disney, *staring* Hayley Mills, and into a BBC production a few years later. The word *Pollyanna* even became a part of the American vocabulary, being listed in Webster's as "someone who is excessively happy."

That's where the problem lies. When we think of a *Pollyanna* now, we think of someone who is foolishly optimistic or excessively happy, someone who denies reality. But the book doesn't really present Pollyanna in that light. It tells of a little girl whose father, a minister, died, leaving her orphaned. Her only relative was an unpleasant and severe aunt in Vermont who took her in. But Pollyanna was an optimist who somehow managed to find a bright side to everything. Her favorite word was "glad," and she was always playing her "Glad Game," a technique she had learned from her father of trying to find something in every situation, no matter how bad, to be glad about.

For example, when she arrived in Vermont, she thought that the servant who met her was her aunt. "Oh, Aunt Polly, I'm so glad you've come to meet me!"

"But I'm not your Aunt Polly," said the servant. "She stayed home." After taking a moment to absorb that, Pollyanna beamed and replied, "Well, I'm glad Aunt Polly didn't come to meet me—because now I can still look forward to meeting *her* and I have *you* for a friend besides!"

Pollyanna's cheerfulness eventually began to transform her aunt into a pleasant and loving person, and in fact, the whole town became a different place because of Pollyanna, just like the verse says: *A cheerful look brings joy to the heart.*

But the real question of the book is—what was behind Pollyanna's optimism?

Like much of earlier fiction, *Pollyanna* was written from a Christian perspective, and there's a very tender chapter in the middle of the book in which the town minister is discouraged to the point of resignation. Things hadn't gone well at church, and people were critical and divided. He rode into the forest to ponder things, but his spirits were lower than they've ever been. Pollyanna, playing in the woods, saw him and noticed his depressed expression.

"I know how you feel," she said as they talked. "Father used to feel like that too, lots of times. I reckon ministers do—most generally. (My father) grew mighty discouraged until he found his rejoicing texts."

"His what?"

"Well, that's what father used to call 'em. Of course, the Bible didn't name 'em that. But it's all those that begin, 'Be glad in the Lord,' or 'Rejoice greatly,' or 'Shout for joy,' and all that, you know—such a lot of 'em. Once, when father felt specially bad, he counted 'em. There were eight hundred of 'em."

"Eight hundred!"

"Yes—that told you to rejoice and be glad, you know; that's why father named 'em the 'rejoicing texts.' Father said that if God took the trouble to tell us eight hundred times to be glad and rejoice, He must want us to do it. And father felt ashamed that he hadn't done it more. After that, they got to be such a comfort to him, you know, when things went wrong, like the time the Ladies' Aiders got in a fight. Why, it was those texts, too, father said, that made him think of the Glad Game."

Thus we learn that Pollyanna's cheerfulness wasn't really an air-headed escape from reality into the fanciful world of positive thinking. It was instead a simple childlike faith, learned from her father, trusting God and rejoicing in all life's ins-and-outs and ups-and-downs. ঙ

43

How to Start a Revival

❦

The world's foremost authority on the subject of revivals and awakenings was the late Dr. J. Edwin Orr, scholar, historian, associate of Billy Graham, and author of numerous books on the subject of spiritual awakenings and revivals.

As a student at Columbia Bible College in the early 1970s, I had read some of Dr. Orr's books, and you can imagine my excitement when I learned he was going to speak on campus.

His lectures were wonderful and inspiring, and I wanted a little time with him personally. Since he was staying overnight in my dormitory, an interview wasn't hard to arrange, but when I met with him, I got the feeling I was inconveniencing him. He wouldn't even look at me, but gazed straight ahead and answered all my questions in short, non-conversational answers as if I weren't there.

Deciding this was just his personality, I sought to bring my interview to a quick conclusion with a final question. "Dr. Orr," I said, "besides praying for revival, what can I do to help start one?"

His answer was worth the stress of the whole appointment, for I've never forgotten it. Looking me straight in the eye at last, the great teacher said simply: "You can let it begin with you, of course." ॐ

44

To God Be the Glory

❧❦❧

The hymns *To God Be the Glory, Blessed Assurance, All the Way My Savior Leads Me,* and *He Hideth My Soul* remind us that it's never too late to begin serving Christ. Some people start as children, others as teens or young adults. But Moses was eighty when God commissioned him, and Paul was middle-aged.

So was Fanny Crosby, author of the above hymns.

Fanny was born in a cottage in South East, New York, in 1820. Six weeks later, she caught a cold in her eyes, and a visiting doctor prescribed mustard poultices, leaving her virtually blind for life. Growing into childhood, she determined to make the best of it, writing at age eight: *O what a happy soul I am! Although I cannot see, I am resolved that in this world contented I will be.*

Fanny spent many years in New York's Institution for the Blind, first as a student then as a teacher and writer-in-residence. Her career flourished, her fame swelled. She recited her poems before Congress and became friends with the most powerful people in America, including presidents.

But not until 1851 did Fanny met her greatest friend, the Lord Jesus. While attending a revival meeting at John Street Methodist Church in New York, she later recalled, a prayer was offered, and "they began to sing the grand old consecration hymn, 'Alas! And Did My Savior Bleed?' and when they reached the line, 'Here, Lord, I give myself away,' my very soul was flooded with celestial light."

Fourteen years later she met the hymnist William Bradbury who told her, "Fanny, I thank God we have met, for I think you can write hymns." Bradbury suggested an idea for a song he needed, and on February 5, 1864, Fanny Crosby, seizing his idea, wrote:

> _We are going, we are going,_
> _To a home beyond the skies,_
> _Where the fields are robed in beauty_
> _And the sunlight never dies._

It was her first hymn, and she was forty-four. But by the time she reached her "home beyond the skies" fifty years later, she had written eight thousand more.

We often overestimate what we can accomplish during the first half of our lives while badly underestimating the impact of the last half of our lives. It isn't physical energy but spiritual maturity that leaves the greatest mark. Our best days of service are always yet to come. ⁊

45

The 1908 World Series

❦

The 1908 National League season saw a fierce struggle between the Chicago Cubs and New York Giants. When they met with the Pennant on the line, there was a last minute change in the Giant lineup. The Giant's first baseman had a sprained back, and substituting for him was an eager nineteen-year-old named Fred Merkle who was thought to be a rising star in baseball.

The game was tied, and in the bottom of the ninth, the Giants were at bat. There were two outs, and two men on base. The winning run was on third, and Fred Merkle was on first. The batter hit a single, and the runner on third lumbered home. The Giants had apparently won the game and the pennant. Jubilant Giant fans poured onto the field while Fred Merkle was still on his way to second. Alarmed by the crowd suddenly bearing down on him and convinced the game was over, he ran straight for the clubhouse.

He didn't go all the way to second base. The Chicago second baseman noticed the Merkle hadn't bothered to touch second. If he could get the ball and touch second himself, the winning run would be cancelled by the force-out. First he had to find the ball.

One of the New York coaches saw what was happening, and he ran for the ball and threw it into the stands. A fan in a brown bowler caught it and started home with his trophy. Two Cubs players chased the man through the mob and tried to take the ball away from him. When he resisted, they knocked him down, grabbed the ball, ran back to the field, and threw it to their second baseman, who, holding the ball, jumped up and down on the bag to make sure the umpire saw what he had done.

As a result, New York lost the game—and the Pennant—and although Fred Merkle stuck it out for fourteen more years in baseball, he never got over the reputation of being the man responsible for what is still to this day called "Merkle's Boner."

A lot of people think they're safe, think they're headed home, think they're going to heaven—but they haven't touched the base.

Jesus once said, "Not everyone who says to Me, 'Lord, Lord,' shall enter the kingdom of heaven, but he who does the will of My Father in heaven."

"Examine yourselves as to whether you are in the faith," said the Apostle Paul in 2 Corinthians 13:5–6. "Test yourselves. Do you not know yourselves, that Jesus Christ is in you?—unless indeed you are disqualified. But I trust that you will know that we are not disqualified." ૐ

46

Patience

❧❧❧

The popular writer F. W. Boreham once lost patience with a difficult man named Crittingden, who said and wrote many critical words. Boreham, angered beyond endurance, finally wrote a flaming letter designed to sting and rebuke the complainer. He walked to the mailbox to post the letter. It was a lovely night for a walk, and he passed by the mailbox without dropping the letter in. He said to himself, "I'll mail it on the way back."

A quarter of a mile further on, he met a friend who said, "Poor old Crittingden is dead."

Boreham was shocked. "Is he, indeed? When did this happen?"

"Oh, he died suddenly early this afternoon. It's really for the best, you know. He's had a hard time. You know all about it, I suppose?"

"No, I don't."

"Oh, I thought everybody knew. He only had two children, a son and a daughter. The son was killed soon after his wife died, and the daughter lost her mind and is in the asylum. Poor old Crittingden never got over it. It soured him."

Boreham returned to his fireside that night, humbled and ashamed. He tore the letter into small fragments and burned them one by one. And as he kneeled before the blaze, he prayed that he, in days to come, might find the grace to deal gently and lovingly with difficult people, even as he wished they might have the grace to treat him.

Stephen Covey writes in his *Seven Habits of Highly Effective People* about an experience he had on a subway in New York. It was Sunday morning, and the passengers were sitting quietly, napping, reading the paper, some lost in thought. But the peaceful scene changed when a man and his children suddenly boarded. The children were loud and rambunctious, and they disrupted the entire car.

The man sat down beside Covey, seemingly oblivious to the situation. The children were yelling, throwing things, and even grabbing people's papers. It was very disturbing, and yet the man did nothing.

Covey fought the feelings of irritation that rose in

him, but as the confusion grew worse he finally turned and said, "Sir, your children are really disturbing a lot of people. I wonder if you couldn't control them a little more?"

The man lifted his gaze as if coming to himself, then he said softly, "Oh, you're right. I guess I should do something about it. We just came from the hospital where their mother died about an hour ago. I don't know what to think, and I guess they don't know how to handle it either."

Covey later wrote, "Can you imagine what I felt at that moment? My paradigm shifted. Suddenly I saw things differently, and because I saw differently, I thought differently, I felt differently, I behaved differently. My irritation vanished . . . my heart was filled with the man's pain. Feelings of sympathy and compassion flowed freely . . . Everything changed in an instant."* &

---

*Adapted from Stephen R. Covey, *The 7 Habits of Highly Effective People,* (New York: Simon and Schuster). 30–31.

47

No Hopeless Cases

⋙❧⋘

Never stop praying for "hopeless" cases, for there are none. No one is beyond the Lord's ability to convict and convert.

Consider the example of E. Howard Cadle. His mother was a Christian, but his father was an alcoholic. By age twelve, Cadle was emulating his father, drinking and out of control. Soon he was in the grip of sex and gambling and in the clutches of the Midwest crime syndicate.

"Always remember, Son," his worried mother often said, "that at eight o'clock every night I'll be kneeling beside your bed, asking God to protect my precious boy." But her prayers didn't seem to slow him until one evening on a rampage, he pulled a gun on a man and squeezed the trigger. The weapon never fired and someone quickly knocked it away. Cadle noticed that it was exactly eight o'clock, and somehow he'd been spared from committing the crime of murder.

He continued headlong in vice, however, and presently his health broke. The doctor told him he had only six months to live. Dragging himself home, penniless and pitiful, he collapsed in his mother's arms, saying, "Mother, I've broken your heart. I'd like to be saved, but I've sinned too much."

The old woman opened her Bible and read Isaiah 1:18—*Though your sins are like scarlet, They shall be as white as snow.* That windswept morning, March 14, 1914, E. Howard Cadle started life anew. The change in him was dramatic and permanent.

With Christ now in his heart, he turned his con skills into honest pursuits and started making money hand over fist, giving 75 percent of it to the Lord's work. He helped finance the crusades of the far-famed evangelist Gipsy Smith in which thousands were converted. Then he began preaching the Gospel himself on Cincinnati's powerful WLW, becoming one of America's earliest and most popular radio evangelists.

He once said: *Until He calls me, I shall preach the same Gospel that caused my sainted mother to pray for me. And when I have gone to the last city and preached my last sermon, I want* to sit at His feet and say, "Thank You, Jesus, for saving me that dark and stormy day from a drunkard's and a gambler's Hell." ❧

48

Another Mother's Prayers

⌘

When we don't know what to do, we can pray, asking God for wisdom and, when necessary, His intervening hand.

Francis and Edith Schaeffer, missionaries to Switzerland, began a powerful ministry out of their home. It was called L'Abri, and many university students and intellectuals found there the answers they were seeking for the great questions of life. Francis Schaeffer's lectures and books earned him the title "Missionary to the Intellectuals."

Early in their ministry, when they returned from America to their Swiss home, young Franky grew ill and lost his ability to walk. The doctor diagnosed polio, and Edith, greatly distressed, devoted her waking hours to caring for him while her husband resumed his widespread traveling ministry.

Francis was in Italy when Franky suffered a severe attack. There were limited medical facilities in their small Swiss village, and when the local doctor arrived, he had with him a virtually-untested serum he himself had invented. "Please let me use it," he begged Edith. "Don't deny the boy the possibility of help. He may never walk again otherwise."

Edith, sick with panic, silently cried, "Oh Father, show me what is best. I'll go with the doctor unless you stop me, God. I don't know what else to do." Meanwhile the doctor paced the floor, saying, "Hurry, hurry . . . no time to lose." Jumping in the car they raced to the little hospital. The ether mask was affixed over Franky's screaming face, and the injection given, with another scheduled for the morning.

Edith later wrote: *I became increasingly frightened about it. But in the early morning as I was reading my Bible beside Franky, a verse in Proverbs suddenly hit me. "The king's heart is in the hand of the Lord, as the rivers of water: He turneth it whithersoever He will." I thought, "If God can turn a king's heart the way He can turn the course of a river, surely God can turn the decision of this doctor in the direction best for Franky," and as I asked God to do this, I stopped trembling. The doctor walked in with a nurse and as she started to pull the cot towards the operation room, the doctor put up his hand and said sharply, "Wait." Then he gazed at Franky a few minutes and finally said, "I've changed my mind. We won't do it." The second injection was never given.*

Whatever that injection did, Franky did not have any paralysis, and the day came when he could sit up, then stand, and finally walk. * ⧽*

---

*Adapted from Edith Schaeffer, *L'Abri* (Wheaton, IL: Tyndale House Publishers, 1969). 65–71.

49

Two Becoming One

❦

O ne of my favorite writers through the years has been Isobel Kuhn, author and missionary to China and Thailand with Overseas Missionary Fellowship (OMF), who died of breast cancer when she was fifty-five.

Isobel grew up in a Christian family, and after a period of doubt and waywardness, gave herself to the Lord for ministry and enrolled at the Moody Bible Institute of Chicago. There she met John Kuhn, who was to become her husband. Both were deeply committed to Christ and to missions, but both were extremely strong-willed and opinionated. They often clashed.

Their worst fight was caused by a cook in China to whom John was devoted. Isobel couldn't stand this man and she often had words with him, and with John. As tensions grew, Isobel sulked and stewed and finally exploded.

To her shock, instead of firing this cook, John sided with him.

Isobel, enraged beyond endurance, put on her hat and coat and walked out of the house, through the town, onto the plain boiling with rage. She said to herself, "I am not going to live with a man who gives a lazy servant preference over the wife."

She walked for hours, enraged, not caring where she went. She finally returned home—where else could she go?—but the situation remained tense until John told Isobel she could dismiss the servant. To make matters worse, the local church leaders paid the couple a visit to know why the cook had been fired.

John wouldn't back Isobel, and she was left trying to explain the situation to an unsympathetic audience. Furthermore, John didn't hire anyone to replace the cook, and all the domestic duties fell on Isobel.

Other issues arose, and for a long time the Kuhn's marriage was painful and stressed. But John and Isobel were committed to the Master and to continued personal spiritual maturity. They were committed to working on their relationship, however difficult it seemed. Their marriage overcame the obstacles, making them a powerful missionary couple in the Lord's service, utterly devoted to Christ and to each other.

Near the end of her life, Isobel wrote these words: _I feel many modern marriages are wrecked on sharp shoals just as this. A human weakness is pointed out. The correction is resented. Argument grows bitter. Young people are not ready to forgive, not willing to endure. Divorce is too quickly seized upon as the way out. [But] to pray God to awaken the other person, to be patient until He does so—this is God's way out. And it molds the two opposite natures into one invincible whole._

That is the miracle of marriage. ❧

50

A Dose of Compassion

❦

Byron Deel grew up with an alcoholic and abusive father. Byron had two brothers and three sisters, a large family, but his dad spent the family income on alcohol, and he drank and ranted and raved and cursed and threatened and hit them. And then he left them. When Byron was twelve, his father walked away from the family, and did absolutely nothing to support them. There were no child care payments. No alimony. No cards at birthdays. No gifts at Christmas. Nothing but hardship and abandonment.

Six years later, he showed up again, two weeks after Byron had graduated from high school. It was an awkward meeting. He stayed about half an hour. And then he left again, and this time there was no contact for sixteen years. Byron told me, "My attitude toward my dad was everything that it shouldn't have been for a Christian. He had robbed me of a happy childhood. He had failed me at every point. He had abused me. I hesitate to say that I hated him, but perhaps hatred isn't too strong a word. There was a bitterness there that was almost a loathing. Whenever anyone asked me about my dad, I'd shut them off pretty fast. As I grew older, I put it all out of my mind, and there was just a blank spot there. I didn't think about it. I could go for years without once thinking about my father."

One day out of the blue his father's sister called Byron and said, "Your father is in Bristol, Virginia, very sick and close to death. It would mean something to him if he could see one of his children. He has cirrhosis of the liver." None of the other children wanted to see him, and Byron lived the closest to Bristol. So he got in his car and drove up there. He said, "I had a ton of thoughts. Not a lot of strong feelings, just a sense that someone should do this. I didn't want to, but it seemed like I should."

Byron walked into the Intensive Care Unit and there was a seventy-one-year old man, connected to monitors, tubes inserted into his body, surrounded by medical equipment. Byron had not seen him for sixteen years, but he recognized the man. And something strange happened. As Byron saw his father lying there helplessly, dying, strung about with wires and tubes and monitors and machines, all the years of hatred and anger melted away. He walked over and stood by the bedside. The man opened his eyes, saw Byron, and began to cry.

Byron said, "I wept, too. It was almost as though I could see going through his mind waves of regret for the wasted years." Byron spent that day and the next with his dad, and he was surprised to find that he had a lot of feeling for the man. "The burden that I had been carrying around for years without realizing it, it was gone. We were able to talk, and I was able to share the gospel with him."

Byron's father survived that stay in the hospital, and was able to return home briefly. During that time, Byron had a second visit, taking his wife and daughters with him. And during that visit, he grew convinced that his dad had trusted Jesus Christ as his Lord and Savior.

Later the call came that he had died, but Byron was no longer bitter or estranged. The compassion of Jesus Christ had taken hold, and instead of seeing himself as an abused victim full of hatred and cold of heart, he saw something else. He saw his dad through the Lord's eyes, as a needy man who just needed Jesus Christ.

Henry Wadsworth Longfellow once wrote, "If we could only read the secret history of our enemies, we would find in each man's life sorrow and suffering enough to disarm all hostility." ❧

51

Out of China

❦

We never face any life-situation for which God has not supplied specific promises that give us mercy and grace to help in time of need. The old Puritan Thomas Watson put it very quaintly in a sermon to his little congregation in England on Sunday, August 17, 1662: *Trade much in the promises. The promises are great supports to faith. Faith lives in a promise, as the fish lives in the water. The promises are both comforting and quickening, the very breast of the gospel; as the child by sucking the breast gets strength, so faith by sucking the breast of a promise gets strength and revives. The promises of God are bladders (flotation devices) to keep us from sinking when we come to the waters of affliction. O! trade much in the promises, there is no condition that you can be in, but you have a promise.*

One couple's story proves the point. Arthur and Wilda Mathews were among the nearly one thousand missionary personnel with China Inland Mission who were trapped in China when the Communists took over in the late 1940s. CIM ordered a total evacuation in January, 1951, but was it was too late? The communists were not adverse to killing.

The Mathews applied for exit visas on January 3, but were put off. Their living conditions had deteriorated to a bare kitchen where, in the corner, Wilda had converted a footlocker into a prayer nook. Days passed with no action on their requests. Meanwhile citizens were executed every day, and from her kitchen Wilda could hear the shots, and she didn't know when they might be next. The strain grew unbearable. "The imagination jumps around into all sorts of places it ought to keep out of," Arthur wrote to his parents.

He was told at last that his wife and child could leave if he would secretly work for the Communists. Arthur refused. Day after day he was summoned and grilled. Day after day he said good-bye to Wilda, wondering if he would ever see her again. Finally Arthur bluntly told the authorities, "I am not a Judas. If you expect me or anyone else in the China Inland Mission to do that kind of thing, you had better not try because we cannot do it."

Wilda was utterly overcome by fear and doubt. Sunday, March 21, 1951, was, as she called it later, Black Easter. Wilda sneaked into an Easter church service, but when she opened her mouth to sing "He Lives!" no words came out. Returning home, she fell at the trunk and her trembling fingers found 2 Chronicles 20:17, the very promise she desperately needed from God: *You will not need to fight in this battle. Position yourselves, stand still and see the salvation of the Lord, who is with you . . . Do not fear.*

Wilda clamped onto that verse, and two weeks later she wrote, "The conflict has been terrible, but peace and quiet reign now."

It was two years before she exited the country, and even longer for Arthur who became the last CIM missionary to leave China. But miraculously, all of them got out without a single one being martyred. It was the greatest exodus in missionary history.

J. I. Packer wrote in his book *Knowing God: In the days when the Bible was universally acknowledged in the churches as "God's Word written," it was clearly understood that the promises recorded in Scripture were the proper, God-given basis for all our life of faith, and that the way to strengthen one's faith was to focus it upon particular promises that spoke to one's condition.*

We don't have to be wobbly and weak-kneed when standing on God's promises. He has promised to fulfill every one. ❧

52

Disappointments Are His Appointments

❦

Mike Holmgren was raised in a church-going, Swedish-American family in a second-floor flat above his grandfather's bakery, a stone's throw from Candlestick Park, the home of the San Francisco 49ers. At an early age he caught football fever. In high school, Mike was chosen all-American quarterback. In college, he played for UCLA, dreaming of a career in the NFL. His excitement was unbounded in 1970 when he was drafted by the St. Louis Cardinals. But he was cut during the preseason. Then the New York Jets considered him as Joe Namath's backup, but later went with another player.

I was crushed. All that had mattered to me was playing pro football, and now that would never happen. The flight home from New York was the longest five hours of my life. I felt like a failure.

Returning home, Mike retreated to his bedroom in depression, but there found his old, dust-covered Bible. He had become a Christian at age eleven, but in his intense pursuit of football, he had forgotten the Lord. Now as he thumbed through the Bible, he found a verse he had once memorized in Sunday School: "Trust in the Lord with all your heart, And lean not on your own understanding; In all your ways acknowledge Him, And He shall direct your paths."

Mike recommitted his life to Jesus Christ. Shortly afterward, he fell in love with a girl who had just returned from a missionary stint in Zaire. They were married, and Mike began coaching at his high school alma mater. He has been coaching ever since, becoming one of the most successful NFL coaches in America as head coach of the Green Bay Packers.

"Win or lose," Mike says, "I now realize what really matters: It's not the Super Bowl rings—it's the crown of eternal life that Jesus Christ has won for us through His victory on the cross.* ॐ

---

*Adapted from Mike Holmgren as told to Greg Asimakoupoulos, "What Matters Most in My Life," *Decision*, October 1997, 8–9.

53

A Father's Lesson

৵৻ৡৡ৵

W hile family devotions are important, the most effective sharing is spontaneous. Children learn best when parents convey the Scriptures naturally and frequently, *when you sit in your house, when you walk by the way, when you lie down, and when you rise up.* (Deuteronomy 6:7).

For example, Robert Webber, a professor of theology, grew up on the mission field where his parents served the Africa Inland Mission. Once on furlough, the young family settled in Montgomery, Pennsylvania, in a small home near a farm. Robert was nine years old, and he loved blackberries. One day he grabbed a bucket and started picking blackberries on nearby bushes. Without thinking, he strayed onto the neighbor's property and started picking the farmer's crop.

Suddenly, the neighbor burst out the front door, waving his fist. "Get out of my field!" he shouted. "And don't let me catch you on my property ever again! Do you understand me?"

Robert was terrified, and he quickly ran to tell his father. Mr. Webber said, "Give me that pail of blackberries. We're going next door to talk to that man." The two marched across the yard, Robert thinking to himself, "Good! My dad will show him a thing or two!"

"Mr. Farmer," said Robert's dad. "I'm sorry my son was on your property. Here, I want you to have these blackberries."

The neighbor was completely disarmed. "Hey," he said, "I'm sorry I yelled at the boy. I don't want the blackberries. I don't even like blackberries. You keep them. And you can pick all the berries you want from my field."

As we walked back home, Dad turned to me and said, "The Scripture says, 'A soft answer turns away wrath.' Remember that, Robert." I've not always lived up to that Scripture, or to the example of my father, but I've never forgotten those words or my dad's action that gave those words meaning. ❋ ⊱

_____

*Adapted from Dr. Robert Webber, "A Father's Influence," *What My Parents Did Right,* comp. and ed. Gloria Gaither, (Nashville: Star Song Publishing Group, 1991). 207–208.

54

Providential Orderings at the English Channel

❦

King Philip II of Spain, a 16th century Catholic monarch, wanting to topple Protestantism in England, readied his navy, the largest and strongest on earth, for invasion. He was trusting God, he said, to send him favorable weather, as he would be fighting a divine cause. On May 30, 1588 he fell to his knees before his "Invincible Armada," prayed for victory, and watched it disappear over the horizon.

But providence sided with Queen Elizabeth I and the English. The Spanish Armada was quickly hurled in every direction by a violent storm. The beleaguered fleet regrouped, pressed on, and was spotted by the British on July 19. Winds turned against the Armada, slowing its progress.

When the battle was joined on July 21, weather again aided the English. Heavy winds favored their smaller, more manageable ships. The English outmaneuvered the Spanish, and at just the right moments the weather shifted, always in England's favor.

By July 31, the Duke of Parma had informed Philip of likely defeat: "God knows how grieved I am at this news at a time when I hoped to send Your Majesty congratulations. I will only say that this must come from the hand of the Lord, who knows well what He does . . ."

A week later, Queen Elizabeth visited her military headquarters at Tilbury and was told there that the danger of invasion was past. The relieved queen addressed her forces, saying: _I know that I have the body of a weak and feeble woman, but I have the heart and stomach of a king._

Philip's tattered ships, limping back to Spain, were caught in another deadly squall. Less than half the vessels and a third of the troops survived the storms and battles. But back in London, the Queen went to St. Paul's Cathedral and "with her own princely voice, she most christianly urged the people to give thanks unto God."

Centuries later, another ominous threat faced England across the Channel. Poland, Denmark, Norway, Holland,

Belgium, France—all had fallen to the Nazi blitzkrieg, forcing the British Expeditionary Force to the sea and trapping them for apparent, inevitable annihilation.

England's King George VI called for a national day of prayer as a risky evacuation began on May 26, lasting for ten days. The weather behaved oddly. When the dikes were opened to hinder the German advance, the wind blew in from the sea, aiding this strategic move. But had it continued to blow in from the sea, it would have wrecked many of the tiny boats and small vessels transporting soldiers. Instead, the wind blew as needed, where needed, and when needed to facilitate the retreat. And when not needed, it didn't blow.

Thousands of troops escaped in an improvised flotilla of tiny vessels only because, through the entire evacuation, the waters of the English Channel were as still as a pond, despite the fact that at the end of May the channel is normally rough and stormy. As an added advantage, the fog rolled in at critical moments, covering the rescue of the troops.

It is called to this day the "Miracle of Dunkirk."

The quaint Puritan, Thomas Watson, once wrote: *There is no such thing as blind fate, but there is a Providence that guides and governs the world. "The lot is cast into the lap, but its every decision is from the Lord* (Proverbs 16:33) . . . *Providence is God's ordering all issues and events of things, after the counsel of His will, to His own glory . . .* ❧

55

Christ, Who Is Your Life

❧⸾❧

During World War II, Major Ian Thomas served with the British Expeditionary forces in Belgium and took part in the evacuation at Dunkirk. He later became a far-famed evangelist and Bible teacher, and the founder of Capernwray Missionary Fellowship and its chain of Torch-bearers Schools.

Despite the drama of his military career, the defining moment for Ian Thomas really came when he was a young man at the university. He was leader of the InterVarsity Fellowship group on his campus in London, and he poured himself into campus evangelism with incredible zeal. He later recalled, "Out of a sheer desire to win souls, to go out and get them, I was a windmill of activity, until, at the age of nineteen, every moment of my day was packed tight with doing things: preaching, talking, counseling.

"The only thing that alarmed me was that nobody

was converted! That gets a little discouraging after a bit, doesn't it? The more I did, the less happened, and it was not a question of insincerity. The prospects and the environment were good; there was plenty of ammunition and plenty of target, but just nothing happened! I became deeply depressed because I really loved the Lord Jesus Christ with all my heart; I wanted to be made a blessing to my fellow men. But I discovered that forever doubling and redoubling my efforts, rushing here and dashing there, taking part in this campaign, taking part in that campaign, preaching in the morning, preaching in the evening, talking to the Bible class, witnessing to this one, counseling with another, did nothing, nothing to change the utter barrenness and uselessness of my activity.

"Thus by the age of nineteen, I had been reduced to a state of complete exhaustion spiritually, until I felt that there was no point in going on."

But one night in November of that year, Ian Thomas, about midnight, got down on his knees in his room and wept in sheer despair. "Oh, God," he said, "I know that I am saved. I love Jesus Christ. I am perfectly convinced that I am converted. With all my heart I have wanted to serve Thee. I have tried to my uttermost and I am a hopeless failure!"

Suddenly a phrase from a Bible verse flashed into Thomas' mind: *Christ, who is your life!* It hit him with terrific force and it seemed God was saying this to him: "For seven years with utmost sincerity, you have been trying to live *for* Me, on My behalf, the life that I have been waiting for seven years to live *through* you. Now supposing I am your life . . . I am your strength . . . I am your victory in every area of life."

And Ian Thomas relinquished his own role in his own life, saying to the Lord: "If this is true, then I am going to thank Thee for it in sheer cold-blooded faith, with no evidence to support it, and nothing but a history of failure behind me. I am going to thank Thee that if Thou art my life, and this is true, then Thou art my strength, Thou art my power, Thou art my future. Thou art the One Who is going to go out now, clothed with me, to do all that I so hopelessly have been trying to do in the past seven years."

Shortly after, Thomas was to speak to a boys' Bible class. On his way, he said, "Well now, Lord, Thou art going to speak to that boys' class, isn't it wonderful? Yesterday I thought I was going to, but Thou art going to now!"

He arrived to find about ninety boys gathered for the class. He just spoke simply about the Lord Jesus, then invited any who wanted to receive Him as Lord and Savior to see him afterward. Thirty boys stayed behind. And that was the beginning of an extraordinary lifetime of fruitful ministry.

It isn't what we do for Christ that counts. It's what He does in and through us, even as the Apostle Paul wrote in Romans 15:18: "For I will not dare to speak of anything except what Christ has accomplished through me to lead the Gentiles to obedience by word and deed" (New American Bible). &

56

Touch of the Master's Hand

❧❦❧

O ne of the most famous musicians of the 19th Century was a self-taught Norwegian violinist named Ole Bull (1810½1880). He was a composer and artist of amazing skill who toured Europe and America with enormous success. During his lifetime, he was the world's most renowned violinist.

But he wasn't known by everyone. One day while traveling in the forests of Europe, he became lost and in the dark of night stumbled upon a log hut, the home of a hermit. The old man took him in, fed and warmed him, and after supper they sat in front of a blazing fireplace and the old hermit picked some crude tunes on his screechy, battered violin.

"Do you think I could play on that?" asked Ole Bull.

"I don't think so," replied the hermit. "It took me years to learn."

Ole Bull replied, "Let me try." Taking the old marred violin, he drew the bow across the strings and suddenly the hermit's hut was filled with music so beautiful the hermit sobbed like a child.

We are battered instruments; life's strings have been snapping; life's bow has been bent. Yet if we will only let Him take us and touch us, from this old battered, broken, shattered, marred instrument, He will bring forth music fit for the angels.

All it takes is the touch of the Master's hand. ૨૭

57

Here's Me!

❧

Think of what you were when you were called, *said Paul.* Not many of you were wise, influential, or of noble birth. But God chose the lowly things *. . .* (1 Corinthians 1:26–27 NIV) It had started on a bus in England. Gladys Aylward, a poorly-educated twenty-eight-year-old parlor maid, was reading about China and the need for missionaries there, and from that moment, China became her life and passion. She applied to a missionary agency only to be turned down. Crushed with disappointment, she returned to her small servant's room and turned her pocketbook upside down. Two pennies fell on top of her Bible. "O God," she prayed, "here's my Bible! Here's my money! Here's me!"

Gladys began hoarding every cent to purchase passage to China. She knew she couldn't afford to travel by ship, so she decided to go overland by train right across Europe and Asia, though it meant slicing through a dangerous war zone on the Manchurian border. On October 15, 1932, a little bewildered party gathered at London's Liverpool Street Station to see Gladys Aylward off for China. The journey was hair-raising and nearly cost her life. But eventually Gladys reached China, showing up at the home of an older missionary who took her in—but didn't quite know what to do with her.

And yet—to make a long story short—Gladys Aylward eventually became one of the most amazing single woman missionaries of modern history. Her missions career was so extraordinary that the world finally took notice. Her biography was made into a movie starring Ingrid Bergman. She dined with such dignitaries as Queen Elizabeth and spoke in great churches. She even became a subject of the television program "This is Your Life."

But Gladys never grew accustomed to the limelight, for her heart was always in Asia. "I wasn't God's first choice for what I've done for China," she once said. "There was somebody else . . . I don't know who it was—God's first choice. I don't know what happened. Perhaps he died. Perhaps he wasn't willing. And God looked down . . . and saw Gladys Aylward." ❧

58

Latimer's Light

❦

Many people think the English Reformation occurred in 16th century England because the Pope wouldn't grant a divorce to King Henry VIII, resulting in Henry's breaking relations with Rome.

That isn't entirely true. While King Henry did suspend relations with Rome and declare himself head of the Church of England, he still believed Catholic doctrine and observed Catholic rituals. He just wanted Catholicism without the pope.

The real English Reformation is better credited to a scholar at Cambridge University named Thomas Bilney who embraced reformation truth after reading Erasmus's Greek New Testament.

Bilney, a quiet scholar at Cambridge University, had acquired a Greek New Testament from the famous scholar Erasmus. While pouring over it, he was deeply stirred by one verse of Scripture, 1 Timothy 1:15: *Christ Jesus came into the world to save sinners!*

"This one sentence," he later wrote, "through God's instruction and inward working, did so exhilarate my heart, which before was wounded with the guilt of my sins, that immediately I found wonderful comfort and quietness in my soul. My bruised bones leaped for joy."

Bilney wanted to share his conversion with others, but this was Reformation truth, and despite King Henry's problems with the pope, the Reformation had not yet stirred England. Teachers such as Luther—and teachings like justification by grace through faith—were being fiercely attacked by English churchmen like the young, but powerful and influential, Hugh Latimer.

Bilney listened to young Latimer rail against the Reformation, he prayed an unusual prayer, saying: "O God, I am but 'little Bilney,' and shall never do any great thing for Thee. But give me the soul of that man, Hugh Latimer, and what wonders *he* shall do in Thy most holy name."

One day, breathing a prayer, Bilney pulled Latimer aside, and told him, "Oh, sir, for God's sake, hear my confession." It was a ploy, for as Latimer sat and listened, Bilney spoke Erasmus's Greek New Testament and shared what had happened to him through it. Reaching into his sleeve, he drew out the precious book, and it opened to a passage heavily underlined, 1 Timothy 1:15.

As Latimer read those words, his eyes were opened, and he himself saw the pure and simple truth of the Gospel, that Jesus Christ came into the world to save sinners. The effect on Latimer was reminiscent of the conversion of Saul of Tarsus. Tears poured down his cheeks, and in that moment he was born again.

Soon Latimer was preaching the faith he had once labored to destroy. As a result, he fell from favor during Henry's reign and spent time in the Tower of London. When the more Protestant-leaning King Edward VI came to the throne, Latimer was released for ministry, but when Edward died, Latimer was among those caught and condemned by officials of Queen Mary.

On October 16, 1555, he and Nicholas Ridley were tied back-to-back at the stake in Oxford and set aflame. "Be of good comfort, Mr. Ridley," Latimer cried in words that still echo through Christian history. "Play the man! We shall this day light such a candle, by God's grace, in England, as I trust shall never be put out."

As a result of the courage of "Little Bilney" and his great disciple, Hugh Latimer, the Reformation fires swept over England and, in time, to America.

And the flames leaped up, but the blinding smoke
Could not the soul of Hugh Latimer choke;
For, said he, "Brother Ridley, be of good cheer,
A candle in England is lighted here,
Which by the grace of God shall never go out!" —
And that speech in whispers was echoed about —
Latimer's Light shall never go out,
However the winds may blow it about.
Latimer's Light has come to stay
Till the trump of a coming judging day. * ॐ

_____

*Poem taken from *A Frank Boreham Treasury,* comp. by Peter F. Gunther (Chicago: Moody Press, 1984). 11.

59

Samson

❧❧

My daughter Hannah and I had a Great Dane named Samson whom we dearly loved. But Samson, as it turns out, was well named, for he was big and strong and muscular—and, like his namesake, he had a penchant for wandering. We built fences, we bought enclosures, and we attached him to dog runs. We tried everything to keep Samson at home. But he would always figure out a way to dig under the fence or climb over it, and it drove us to distraction.

It also drove the neighbors to distraction, to look up and see a two-hundred-pound monster running toward them, ears up, tongue out.

Looking for answers, we bought a best-selling book on the market on the subject of training dogs. *No Bad Dogs* was written by the famous British dog trainer Barbara Woodhouse, who raises Great Danes herself. One night when I went upstairs to tuck-in Hannah, she had a sad expression on her face, and she said, "Dad, I know now what Samson's real problem is. Let me read you this paragraph." This is what she read me out of *No Bad Dogs* by Barbara Woodhouse:

In a dog's mind, a master or a mistress to love, honor, and obey is an absolute necessity. The love is dormant in the dog until brought into full bloom by an understanding owner. Thousands of dogs appear to love their owners, they welcome them home with enthusiastic wagging of the tail and jumping up, they follow them about their houses happily and, to the normal person seeing the dog, the affection is true and deep. But to the experienced dog trainer this outward show is not enough. The true test of real love takes place when the dog has got the opportunity to go out on its own as soon as the door is left open by mistake and it goes off and often doesn't return home for hours. That dog loves only its home comforts and the attention it gets from its family; it doesn't truly love the master or mistress as they fondly think. True love in dogs is apparent when a door is left open and the dog still stays happily within earshot of its owner. For the owner must be the be-all and end-all of a dog's life.

I went to my own bedroom sobered, thinking, not about Samson, but about me. It was as though the Lord was telling me that the real test of my Christianity isn't seen in my work or activity, or even in my theological purity as important as that is.

It is found in this: when I have an opportunity to wander away, to disobey, to leave His presence, do I choose instead to stay close to Him, to abide in Christ, to obey? ೋ

60

A Deep Sleep

❦

Imagine surgery before the day of anesthesia. Patients were strapped down while scalpel and saw cut through tissue and bone, every slice and turn of the knife causing unimaginable pain.

One physician determined to do something about it. Sir James Young Simpson (1811½1870) practiced medicine in Scotland. He became Senior President of the Royal Medical Society of Edinburgh when only twenty-four, and in time received virtually every possible honor and position, including being named one of Her Majesty's physicians for Scotland.

Simpson dreamed of finding a way of putting patients to sleep during surgery, for even as a young physician he was horrified at the intense suffering patients endured while under the knife.

In an effort to find some way of reducing the pain

and consciousness of surgery, Simpson periodically invited other learned scientists and physicians to his home to discuss options and ideas. These meetings usually occurred on Monday nights, and often involved experiments with chemicals, crystals, and powders, which were placed over a burning brazier while the doctors inhaled the fumes.

Nothing worked until November 4, 1847. One of the men had purchased a crystal called chloroform in Paris. As the doctors sniffed the burning substance, one after another of them fell to the floor unconscious. When they awoke, they knew they had achieved a powerful medical breakthrough.

Simpson now had his answer, but he soon encountered another problem. Strange as it seems, he was attacked by fellow Christians who claimed that pain was a God-ordained part of life. Freedom from pain comes only in heaven, some of them said, and it is immoral to devise dangerous ways of escaping it on earth.

Sir James, himself a devoted Christian, went to the Scriptures, seeking answers. He no sooner opened his Bible then he came to Genesis 2:21: *And the Lord God caused a deep sleep to fall on Adam, and he slept; and He took one of his ribs, and closed up the flesh in its place.*

Carefully studying the text, Simpson wrote an article

entitled, "Answer to the Religious Objections Advanced Against the Employment of Anesthetic Agents in Midwifery and Surgery."

"In this remarkable verse," Simpson wrote, referring to Genesis 2:21, "the whole process of a surgical operation is briefly detailed, but the passage is principally striking as affording evidence of our Creator Himself using means to save poor human nature from the unnecessary endurance of physical pain."

Simpson then ended his paper saying, "We may rest fully assured that whatever is true on point of fact or humane and merciful in point of practice, will find no condemnation in the Word of God."

His critics were silenced, and a new day dawned in medical science.

Mercy and the Master are never far apart, and when we rightly divide God's Word, His grace shows up in every verse. That's something to be thankful for, even when the anesthesiologist hovers near. ❧

61

All These Things

❧

In *A Turtle on a Fencepost*, Allan Emery tells of accompanying businessman Ken Hansen to visit a hospitalized employee. The patient lay very still, his eyes conveying anguish. His operation had taken eight hours, and recovery was long and uncertain.

"Alex," said Ken quietly, "you know I have had a number of serious operations. I know the pain of trying to talk. I think I know what questions you're asking. There are two verses I want to give you—Genesis 42:36 and Romans 8:28. We have the option of these two attitudes. We need the perspective of the latter."

Hansen turned to the passages, read them, then prayed and left. The young man, Alex Balc, took the message to heart. He later enjoyed full recovery.

Every day we choose one of these attitudes amid life's difficulties—to be beat-up, or to be up-beat. To say with

Jacob in Genesis 42:36: *All these things are against me.* Or to say with Paul in Romans 8:28: *All these things are working together for good to those who love the Lord.* ❧

62

John Paton

John Paton's life was molded by his childhood in a little cottage in Kirkmahoe, Scotland. The cottage had ribs of oak, stone walls, a thatched roof, and three rooms filled with eleven children. The front room served as bedroom, kitchen, and parlor. The rear room was his father's stocking-making shop. The middle room was a closet where John's father retired each day for prayer and Bible study. The sound of his father's prayers through the wall made a powerful impression on young John.

Years later, when Scotland's Reformed Church issued a plea for missionaries for the South Pacific, John went to his parents for advice. They told him something they had never before disclosed—that he had been dedicated to foreign missions before birth.

John sailed from Scotland April 16, 1858, landing on the islands in November. He found himself among cannibals, endangered again and again. "They encircled us in a deadly ring," he wrote of one incident, "and one kept urging another to strike the first blow. My heart rose up to the Lord Jesus; I saw him watching all the scene. My peace came back to me like a wave from God. I realized that my life was immortal till my Master's work with me was done."

For several years, Paton saw little progress, but he persisted in his work. The turning point came when Paton decided to dig a well to provide fresh water for the people. The islanders, terrified at bringing "rain from below," watched with deepest foreboding. Paton dug deeper and deeper until finally, at thirty feet, he tapped into a stream of water. Opposition to his mission work ceased, and the wide-eyed islanders gave him their full respect. Chief Mamokei accepted Christ as Savior, then a few others made the daring step. On October 24, 1869, nearly eleven years after his arrival, Paton led his first communion service. Twelve converted cannibals partook of the Lord's Supper. "As I put the bread and wine into those hands once stained with the blood of cannibalism, now stretched out to receive and partake the emblems of the Redeemer's love," he wrote, "I had a foretaste of the joy of Glory that well nigh broke my heart to pieces."

There was never a parent in the Gospels who came to Christ with a burdened heart and went away empty. God, being a Father, has a special interest in the prayers of parents. When those parents are on their knees, their shadows fall over the world, and their influence extends to the ages. ❧

You Are My Sunshine

❦

L ike any good mother, when Karen found out that another baby was on the way, she did what she could to help her three-year-old son, Michael, prepare for a new sibling. Learning that the new baby was going to be a girl, Karen shared her excitement with little Michael, and day after day, night after night, Michael sang to his sister in Mommy's tummy.

The pregnancy progressed normally for Karen, an active member of the Panther Creek United Methodist Church in Morristown, Tennessee. Then the labor pains came. Every five minutes, then every minute. But complications arose during delivery, and after hours of labor, Michael's little sister was born in a weakened condition. With siren howling in the night, she was rushed by ambulance the neonatal intensive care unit at St. Mary's Hospital in Knoxville, Tennessee.

The baby's condition worsened, and the pediatric specialist told the parents that there was little hope. "Be prepared for the worst," he said. Karen and her husband contacted a local cemetery about a burial plot. They had fixed up a special room in their home for the new baby, but now they found themselves planning a funeral.

Michael, meanwhile, kept begging his parents to let him see his sister, "I want to sing to her," he said.

Another week passed, and the baby was still clinging to life. But barely. Things didn't look good, but Michael kept nagging his mom about singing to his sister. At that time, young children were never allowed as visitors to the Intensive Care Unit, but at length Karen made up her mind to take Michael to see his little sister whether it was allowed or not.

"If he doesn't see his sister now," she said, "he may never see her alive."

Karen dressed him in an oversized scrub suit and took him into ICU looking like a walking laundry basket, but the head nurse recognizes him as a child and bellowed, "Get that kid out of here now! No children are allowed in ICU." Karen, normally a mild-mannered lady, replied, "He is not leaving until he sings to his sister!" and in they marched.

There by his sister's bedside, Michael gazed at the tiny infant who was losing the battle to live. He began to sing to her: _You are my sunshine, my only sunshine, you make me happy when skies are gray._ . . .

Almost at once the baby girl responded. Her pulse rate becomes calm and steady, and Karen said, "Keep on singing, Michael."

He did. _You never know, dear, how much I love you. Please don't take my sunshine away_ . . . The ragged, strained breathing becomes smooth and steady. Healing rest seemed to sweep over the little girl. The nearby nurses began to cry. Karen glowed.

You are my sunshine, my only sunshine. Please don't, take my sunshine away.

Within a short time, the baby was well enough to go home! The medical staff at St. Mary's Hospital called it a miracle.*

And, what did they expect from a God who used a boy's lunch to feed 5000? As David put it in Psalm 8: "You have

---

*This story, originally attributed to _Woman's Day Magazine,_ is all over the internet. Friends who work at Knoxville's St. Mary's Hospital assured me of its truthfulness.

taught the little children to praise you perfectly" (The Living Bible). 🐦

64

Goforth

Perhaps no missionary lived up to his name better than the one called Goforth. Jonathan Goforth, a Canadian by birth, has been called "China's most outstanding evangelist." Missionary historian Ruth Tucker writes, "Of all the missionaries who served in the Orient during the 19th and early 20th centuries, none saw a greater immediate response to his personal ministry than did Jonathan Goforth."

Dr. Charles Trumbull said about him, "God's missionary program for the past half-century would not have been complete without him." Goforth became a powerful evangelist throughout Asia, a rarity for a Westerner, and his crowds sometimes numbered twenty-five thousand people. His Chinese home was open to inquirers—one day alone over two thousand showed up. Multitudes throughout the Orient came to Christ through Jonathan and his wife Rosaline. During his missionary career, fifty Chinese converts went out as ministers or evangelists.

What led Jonathan Goforth overseas?

He came to Christ at age eighteen, and shortly afterward yielded himself to fulltime service after reading Robert Murray M'Cheyne's *Memoirs*. But it was Dr. George Mackay, veteran missionary to Formosa (Taiwan), who drew him to overseas work. Mackay had been traveling across North America for two years trying to recruit young men for Asian evangelism, but he grew bitterly discouraged. One night as Jonathan, a college student at the time, listened, Mackay pronounced himself a failure. All his travels had been in vain, for not one young man had said, "Yes." The missionary had no choice but to return to Formosa alone, without anyone to carry on the work.

Mackay didn't realize it, but his work wasn't in vain after all.

Jonathan later said about that evening: *I heard the voice of the Lord saying: "Who will go for us and whom shall we send?" and I answered: "Here am I, send me." From that hour I became a foreign missionary.* ?❧

65

Answered Prayer for Breakfast

❦

Sophia's husband John Ironside, an ardent soul-winner, spent his short life preaching on the streets, in the parks, in halls and theaters, wherever he could. But at age twenty-seven, he contracted typhoid and quickly died, leaving Sophia with two small boys and no income.

One of the boys, Harry (later the world-famous pastor of Moody Memorial Church), watched his mother closely. On one occasion, he remembered when company came for supper. Sophia's cupboard was nearly bare, but she scraped together a meal with the little that remained. After the visitors left, she found under one of their plates a ten-dollar bill—a vast sum in those days. With eyes full of tears, she offered thanks to God.

Some time later, the cupboard was again empty. Sophia gathered her two sons to the table for breakfast, but their plates were empty, and there was only water to drink. She shared with them a verse of Scripture that had become very meaningful to her, Isaiah 33:16: *He will dwell on high; His place of defense will be the fortress of rocks; Bread will be given him, His water will be sure.*

Bowing her head over the empty plates, she said: "We will give thanks, boys," she said. Closing her eyes, she prayed, "Father, Thou hast promised in Thy Word, 'Your bread shall be given you, and your water shall be sure.' We have the water, and we thank Thee for it. And now, we trust Thee for the bread, or for that which will take its place."

Just as she finished praying, the doorbell rang, and the boys ran to the door to find a man there. "Mrs. Ironside," he said, "I feel very bad. We have been owing you for months for that dress you made for my wife. We've had no money to pay you. But just now we're harvesting our potatoes, and we wondered if you would take a bushel or two on account of the old bill."

"Indeed, I'll be glad to," replied Sophia.

In a few minutes, the potatoes were sizzling in the frying pan, and the boys had answered prayer for breakfast. ✌

66

Blessings in the Library

❧

One day in my Bible study I came to Isaiah 40:31: *But those who wait on the Lord shall renew their strength; They shall mount up with wings like eagles, They shall run and not be weary, They shall walk and not faint.*

It was such a lofty verse that I had trouble getting my hands on what it really meant, on how I could apply it to my own life. It seemed almost too magnificent to contemplate. My insights, and those of the commentaries I consulted, seemed inadequate to covey the grandeur of the passage.

"What did Isaiah mean?" I wondered. "To mount up with wings like eagles? To soar on eagles' wings?" I laid aside my pen, drove to the local library, and spent the afternoon reading up on ornithology, the study of birds.

I learned that most birds fly by flapping their wings. But not eagles. They are built for soaring, not flapping;

that allows them to travel much further on less energy. It seems that God built into our planet invisible columns of hot air called thermals which rise up here and there from the earth's surface. Eagles know where to find thermals. They fly into these invisible updrafts, stretch out their wings, and are lifted higher and higher into the sky as though ascending on an elevator. They may rise as high as 14,000 feet, so high they can not be seen from earth with the naked eye. When they reach those heights, they emerge from the updraft, their wings still spread, and they soar this way and that way, downward and sideward, traveling for miles with very little exertion of strength.

It is a perfect picture. God himself is an invisible, uplifting thermal current. When we claim His promises and trust His Word, we are spreading out the wings of faith and are caught up to a higher plane. We mount up with wings like eagles. We run without growing weary. We walk and do not faint.

The strength we need for holy, effective, victorious living comes not from frantically flapping through the air like sparrows in distress, but from gliding in the currents of God's grace.

How Isaiah knew all this is a mystery, but his theology was as good as his ornithology. ❧

67

Praying Hyde

❦

Isaiah chapter 62 contains this strange suggestion, that we give the Lord no rest, that we "nag" Him in prayer, pleading with such dogged tenacity that God is compelled to respond to our requests. The prophet Isaiah told those who guarded the city of Jerusalem to pray with untiring persistence until God's promises for the city were fulfilled. He put it this way in verses 6 and 7:

I have set watchmen on your walls, O Jerusalem; They shall never hold their peace day or night; You who make mention of the Lord, do not keep silent, And give Him no rest till He establishes and till He makes Jerusalem a praise in the earth.

Once translation says, "They must remind the Lord of His promises . . . They must give Him no rest until He restores Jerusalem."*

---

*Today's English Version

Remind God of His promises? Give Him no rest till He answers? How many of us pray like that?

One man, having studied these verses, did just that, and as a result he was nicknamed "Praying."

John "Praying" Hyde grew up in Carthage, Illinois, in a minister's home. His father's preaching often mentioned the needs of overseas mission fields, and in his pastoral prayers he prayed for labors to be sent forth. At McCormick Theological Seminary, John committed himself to foreign evangelism, and, following graduation, he sailed for Bombay.

John was initially overcome by the difficulties of climate and language. His itinerant ministry took him from village to village, but his preaching produced few converts and he grew discouraged.

Then John Hyde found Isaiah 62:6–7 and took the words as his personal motto. He began praying with remarkable intensity—missing meals, missing meetings, missing preaching appointments, spending days and nights in prayer. And as his prayers went up, revival began to come down upon his labors in India.

At the beginning of 1908, he prayed earnestly to win at least one soul to Christ every day. By December 31, he had recorded over four hundred converts. The following year, the Lord laid two souls per day on his heart, and his prayer was again answered. The next year he prayed for four souls daily with similar results.

Once, stopping at a cottage for water, Praying Hyde pleaded with God for ten souls. He presented the gospel to the family, and by the end of his visit all nine members of the family had been saved. But what of number ten? Suddenly a nephew who had been playing outside ran into the room and was promptly converted.

Hyde's great missionary work flowed from his prayer life like water from a faucet, and he finally wore himself out in prayer, staying on his knees, night after night, year after year, reminding God of his promises and giving the Lord no rest. The great prayer warrior died on February 17, 1912, his last words being: _Bol, Visu Masih, Ki Jah—_ "Shout the victory of Jesus Christ!" ❧

68

Him!

❦

The devotional writer Samuel D. Gordon knew a woman who had memorized much of the Bible, but old age began taking her memory from her. At last, she could only remember one verse of Scripture, 2 Timothy 1:12: *For this reason I also suffer these things; nevertheless I am not ashamed, for I know whom I have believed and am persuaded that He is able to keep what I have committed to Him until that day.*

In time, she began to lose that verse, too, being able to only recall the words: . . . *what I have committed to Him.*

When she came to her deathbed, her loved ones noticed her lips moving. Bending low, they heard her repeating one solitary word over and over: *Him, Him, Him.*

Dr. Gordon noted that she had lost the whole Bible but one word. But in that one word, she had the whole Bible. ❧

69

Don't Give Up

~§⁓

Jesus taught us we should always pray and not lose heart (Luke 18:1).

I have a friend, Yvonne Thigpen, who recently told me how her father became a Christian. While Yvonne was growing up, she knew there were periods of time when her dad was under profound conviction, but he adamantly resisted the gospel. Once, for example, when evangelist Bobby Jackson was conducting a revival in a nearby church, he visited Yvonne's dad and witnessed to him. Her father reacted with hostility, but for two weeks afterward he was sullen and disturbed.

"Yet he never yielded his life to Christ," said Yvonne, "and that just broke our hearts. But we continued praying."

Some years later, Yvonne's mother, a severe diabetic, became ill and lapsed into a coma. She was so bad off that, to everyone's surprise, her husband actually said a prayer, something like this: "Lord, I just can't bear to lose Ruth right now. If you'll spare her life, I'll give you my heart."

Ruth did recover. And Yvonne recalls, "On the first Sunday my mother was able to return to church, my dad went with her and stepped out and gave his heart and life to the Lord Jesus Christ."

How long had Yvonne and others been praying for him? Twenty-five years. "As soon as I accepted the Lord as a child," she said, "I started praying for him. And we prayed twenty-five years."

The famous 19th century philanthropist and evangelist, George Müller, was a prayer warrior who began praying earnestly for a group of five personal friends who were antagonistic toward the gospel. After five years, one of the men came to Christ.

Muller continued praying for the other four, and in ten years, two more were saved. He prayed on for twenty-five years, and the fourth man was converted. For the rest of his life, Muller continued praying for the remaining man, but when he died in 1898, the man was still unsaved. He had prayed for him for fifty-two years.

A few months after Muller's death, the fifth man also found Jesus Christ as his Savior.

D. L. Moody once wrote, *Though we may not live to see the answer to our prayers, if we cry mightily to God, the answer will come.*

Or, as E. M. Bounds, minister and chaplain during the Civil War who wrote eight classic books on prayer, put it: *Prayers are deathless. The lips that uttered them may be closed in death, the heart that felt them may have ceased to beat, but the prayers live before God, and God's heart is set on them and prayers outlive the lives of those who uttered them; outlive a generation, outlive an age, outlive a world . . . Fortunate are they whose fathers and mother have left them a wealthy patrimony of prayer.* ৈ

70

John Harper

❧❦❧

J ohn Harper jostled his luggage while helping Nina, age six, with her suitcase. Harper was a Baptist minister in Glasgow en route to a preaching engagement at Moody Memorial Church of Chicago. His wife had died at Nina's birth, so he was traveling with his young daughter, assisted by Nina's aunt, Miss Jessie Leitch. After settling themselves in the second-class passenger section, they took off to roam the ship. They felt especially fortunate to be on the maiden voyage of the greatest ocean liner ever built—the *Titanic*.

It wasn't Harper's first brush with disaster. When he was two years old, he had fallen into a well and almost drowned. His mother rescued and resuscitated him by holding him by his heels while the water poured out of his lungs. When he was twenty-six, John was swimming in the ocean when he was caught by a riptide and barely fought his way back to shore. At age thirty-two, Harper had found himself aboard a ship in the Mediterranean that was taking on water so rapidly that the crew gave themselves up for lost.

He bore other difficulties, as well. In the summer of 1905, his health broke under the strain of his pastoral labors, and friends grew alarmed at his thin frame and sallow complexion. The next year, his wife, Annie, died, leaving him with tiny Nina.

But Harper was a man of deep faith. "The fear of death did not for one moment disturb me," he said after one of his narrow escapes. "I believed that sudden death would be sudden glory."

John Harper was born into a Christian home on May 29, 1872, and converted at age thirteen. By age eighteen, he knew God had a special mission for him. Though working at the local paper mill, John found himself preaching the gospel to whoever would listen, often standing on street corners after work and proclaiming Christ.

After several years of personal evangelism and street preaching, he was recruited by the Baptists to oversee one of their struggling mission works. Here Harper labored for thirteen years, watching the church grow from twenty-five members to over five hundred, and building a sanctuary that could seat nine hundred. He was known for his intense prayer life. Some nights he would stay at church all night, pleading with God for his hundreds of members by name.

In 1910, Harper was called to Walworth Road Church in London where his preaching skills flourished. The church there grew quickly and souls were added to the kingdom.

Then came an invitation from the Moody Memorial Church of Chicago to preach a special winter series of messages. Harper made the trip with great excitement, and the Lord so blessed his ministry there that he was hardly home when the Moody Church contacted him again, pleading for him to return for a second series of services.

It was a hard decision, for his London flock didn't want to lose their pastor for another three months. One man, Mr. Robert English, pleaded with Harper not to make the trip, saying that while in prayer he had felt an ominous impression of impending disaster. He offered to pay for a new ticket if only Harper would delay his trip. But Harper felt compelled to go. He boarded the Titanic on April 10, 1912.

Four nights into the voyage, Harper stood on deck admiring the sunset. "It will be beautiful in the morning," he said. He was seen later in the evening witnessing to a man; then he went to bed.

In the wee hours, he was jolted awake as the _Titanic_ plowed into a massive iceberg. Quickly wrapping Nina in a blanket, he carried her to the deck and secured a place for her on a lifeboat. When the ship sank, Nina was saved in lifeboat number eleven, sitting on her aunt's lap. For many years, she would not speak of that night, but before her death in 1986, she told of remembering the lights of the ship go out and of hearing the screams of the dying.

But what of her father?

Harper took off his life jacket and gave it to another man, shouting, "Let the women, children, and the unsaved into the lifeboats!" When the _Titanic_ sank, he tumbled into the freezing waters where he perished.

Months later, in a church in Hamilton, Canada, a man rose, saying, "I was on the _Titanic_ the night she went down. I was thrown into the waters and managed to grab a spar and hang on for dear life. The waters were icy. Suddenly a wave brought a man near, John Harper of

Glasgow. He too was holding to a piece of wreckage. He called out, 'Man, are you saved?'

'No, I am not,' I replied.

"He shouted back through the darkness, 'Believe on the Lord Jesus Christ, and thou shalt be saved.'

"The waves bore him away, but a little later he was washed back alongside me. 'Are you saved now?' he called out.

"'No,' I replied.

"'Believe on the Lord Jesus Christ, and thou shalt be saved.' Then losing his hold on the wood, he sank. And there, alone in the night with two miles of water under me, I trusted Christ as my Savior. I am John Harper's last convert." ❧

71

I Was Just Thinking of You

❧❧❧

When Harry Truman became president, he worried about losing touch with common, everyday Americans, so he would often go out and be among them. Those were in simpler days when the President could take a walk around like everyone else. One evening, Truman decided to stroll down to the Memorial Bridge on the Potomac River. When there, he became curious about the mechanism that raised and lowered the middle span of the bridge. He made his way across the cat-walks and through the inner workings of the bridge, and suddenly he came upon the bridge tender, eating his evening supper out of a tin bucket.

The man showed absolutely no surprise when he looked up and saw the best-known and most powerful man in the world. He just swallowed his food, wiped his mouth, smiled, and said, "You know, Mr. President, I was just thinking of you."

It was a greeting that Truman adored and never forgot.

Wouldn't it be wonderful, when Jesus Christ suddenly appears in the clouds, if we could say, "You know, Lord, I was just thinking of you." ❧

72

While She Prayed

❦

What happens when we pray for our children and grandchildren?

Just ask Miriam Harmon of St. Louis. One night in April, 2000, she arrived at the hospital to sit with her eighty-two-year-old mother-in-law, Evelyn Harmon, who was near death. When Miriam entered the room, she knew the end was near, for Evelyn was lying there, not speaking or moving, eyes shut, unresponsive. Miriam was unable to rouse the older woman until she began singing the hymn, "It is Well with My Soul." After the last stanza, Miriam said, "Mom, if it is well with your soul, blink your eyes."

The old woman willed her eyes open and closed three times.

"I knew it was her heart's desire for her children and

grandchildren to come to know the Lord," Miriam later said, "so I decided to pray with her."

Taking her mother-in-law's hand, Miriam began to pray, interceding by name for each of Evelyn's nine children, thirty grandchildren, and sixteen great-grandchildren.

Returning home about 10:30, Miriam went to bed and fell asleep. Later in the night, she was jolted awake by her twenty-one-year-old son, Timothy.

"Mom, wake up! Mom, Mom, I've been in an accident."

"An accident . . . ! Timothy . . . !"

"I'm all right, Mom, but let me tell you what happened."

While Miriam had been at the hospital that evening, Timothy had been a passenger in a car on Highway 40, traveling from St. Louis to East St. Louis. Another car, trying to pass them, cut in too soon, slamming into their left side, propelling them to the right. Then the vehicle behind them plowed into them, spinning them around broadside, and a tow truck traveling in the opposite direction, crashed into them full force.

Timothy first struck the windshield and cracked it open, then he was thrown from the passenger-side window. His shoes, glasses, and watch flew off. He sailed over the guardrails, landed in a patch of grass, and slid into a pond. Looking up, he saw his airborne car coming straight toward him. It landed with a sickening thud one foot away.

"But I'm all right, Mom," he said. "A couple of cuts, that's all."

"Timothy," Miriam said, gathering her wits, "your grandmother and I were praying for you at that very moment."

"I knew it, Mom," he said. "When I landed on that grass and saw that car coming toward me, all I could say was 'Jesus!' I knew you were praying for me. Like you had prayed for Jeremy."

Jeremy was Miriam's teenage son who worked at a car wash. One Wednesday night shortly before, Miriam had been driving home from a prayer meeting at her church, and as she drove, she was fervently praying for her children. She was so engrossed in prayer that she didn't even look up when she passed the car wash to see if Jeremy was there.

Shortly after, Jeremy came home, badly shaken.

"Mom," he said, "I saw you pass by while I was at the car wash."

"I'm sorry, Jeremy. I should have stopped."

"No, let me tell you what happened. At the very moment you passed by, a man had a gun at my head. It was a hold-up. He said, 'Give me your keys and your money.' I said, 'Man, don't do this.' That's when I looked up and saw you pass by.

"When I looked back at the man, he was looking at me strangely, but not really at me. He was sort of looking past me, and it was as though he saw something or someone at my shoulder. All at once, he turned and ran."

"Jeremy," said Miriam. "I was praying for you at that very moment."

"I believe you, Mom," said Jeremy. "I believe you." ❧

73

Default

In a 1975 tennis tournament in Stockholm, Sweden, tennis star Arthur Ashe was playing against Romanian-born Ilie Nastase, who was so ill-tempered he was sometimes called "Nasty" Nastase. He was unusually nasty that day, stalling, cursing, taunting, and acting like a madman. Finally Arthur Ashe put down his racket and walked off the court, saying, "I've had enough. I'm at the point where I'm afraid I'll lose control."

The umpire warned Arthur he was defaulting the match.

"I don't care," replied Ashe. "I'd rather lose that than my self-respect."

The next day the tournament committee met and issued an unexpected announcement. They would have none of Nastase's childish behavior. They insisted that

Nastase default the match for his unsportsman-like conduct and that Ashe be declared the victor.

Arthur Ashe, it was said, won both the game of tennis—and the game of life.*

Proverbs 29:11 says: "A fool gives full vent to his anger, but a wise man keeps himself under control" (New International Version). 🙰

---

*Adapted from an unattributed clipping in my files.

74

I Don't Even Have a Shirt On

⋖⋗

As pastor of one of the largest churches in America, Dr. Adrian Rogers of Memphis has led hundreds of people to faith in Christ, but he still cherishes the memory of his first attempt at soul-winning. He was a teenager in North Carolina, attending an evening church service. The preacher spoke that evening about sharing Christ with others, and he asked the audience, "How many here will promise to be a soul-winner? Who will promise to win a soul for God?" Adrian earnestly raised his hand. He was a new Christian with little training in the Bible, but he sincerely wanted to be a witness for Christ.

Some time later, Adrian, 16, went back to West Palm Beach where he had been raised. One day he was walking to the store wearing only his Levi's—it was a hot day. An old man with white whiskers approached him, needing money. The man admitted, "I've been an old fool. I live on a pension check. When I got my check this time, I cashed it, and a so-called friend of mine and I got drunk. I spent all my check on whiskey. I've been an old fool, and now I don't have any more money."

Adrian said, "Mister, if I had some money, I'd give it to you, but I don't." But as Adrian started to walk away, the Lord spoke to his heart: "Adrian, speak to him about his soul."

Adrian said, "God, I can't speak to him about his soul; I don't even have a shirt on!"

"But Adrian," the Lord seemed to say, "you promised."

"But God, he's a man and I'm a boy!"

"Adrian, you promised."

As Adrian turned back to the man, his heart was racing. But mustering his courage, he said, "Mister, I don't have any money to give you, but I believe I have something better than money. Sir, are you a Christian?"

Tears suddenly streamed from the old fellow's eyes, and his chin started quivering. "No, son," he said, "I'm not a Christian."

"Sir, would you like to be?"

The man replied, "More than anything in this world. If only I knew how to be."

Then Adrian said, "I wish I had a Bible."

"I have one," replied the old man, and he reached into the lining of his old coat and pulled out a little New Testament. Adrian found John 3:16, read it out loud, and explained the verse as well as he could.

"Well, what should I do?" said the old man when Adrian was finished.

"Well, I'm going to pray for you." And as Adrian began praying for the man, he, too, began crying. When he finished, he said, "Sir, you pray now and ask Him to save you." So the old man started to pray through his tears and he asked Jesus to come into his heart, forgive his sin, and save his soul. When he finished his prayer, Adrian asked, "Well, did He do it?"

"I think He did," said the man.

Knowing nothing about follow-up, Adrian thanked the man, wished him well, and turned to leave. But the old fellow called him back. "You man, come back here," he said. "I'm an old man, and I have traveled through almost every state in this country, and you are the first person to ever speak with me about my soul. Thank you, young man, thank you."

And that day, Adrian Rogers walked home leaping and dancing and praising God. He had learned the joy of soul-winning. ॐ

Now Thank We All
Our God

❧❦❧

An old English preacher once said, "A grateful mind is a great mind," and the Bible agrees. There are 138 passages of Scripture dealing with the subject of thanksgiving, and some of them are powerfully worded. Colossians 3:17 is one of my favorites: "And whatever you do in word or deed, do all in the name of the Lord Jesus, giving thanks to God the Father through Him."

And 1 Thessalonians 5:17 says, "In everything give thanks; for this is the will of God in Christ Jesus for you."

Unfortunately there aren't many hymns devoted exclusively to thanking God, but among the small, rich handful we *do* have is *Now Thank We All Our God*. The German Christians sing this hymn like American Christians sing the *Doxology,* considering it to majestically symbolize

ROB MORGAN

their attitude of worship. Yet it's loved on both sides of
the Atlantic and around the world.

Now Thank We All Our God was written by Martin
Rinkart (1586½1649), a Lutheran pastor in the little village
of Eilenberg, Saxony. He grew up as the son of a poor
coppersmith, felt called to the ministry, and after his theological training began his pastoral work just as the Thirty
Years' War was raging throughout Germany.

Floods of refugees streamed into the walled city of
Eilenberg. It was the most desperate of times. The Swedish
army encompassed the city gates, and inside the walls there
was nothing but plague, famine, and fear. Eight hundred
homes were destroyed, and people began dying in increas-
ing numbers. There was a tremendous strain on the pastors, who expended all their strength in preaching the
gospel, caring for the sick and dying, and burying the dead.
One after another, the pastors themselves took ill and perished until at last only Martin Rinkart was left. Some days
he conducted as many as fifty funerals.

Finally the Swedes demanded a huge ransom. It was
Martin Rinkart who left the safety of the city walls to
negotiate with the enemy, and he did it with such courage
and faith that there was soon a conclusion of hostilities,
and the period of suffering ended.

Rinkart knew that there is no emotional healing without thanksgiving and that in every situation in life, there is a reason to be thankful. With that in mind, he composed this hymn for the survivors of Eilenberg, and it has been sung around the world ever since.

Now thank we all our God,
with heart and hands and voices,
who wondrous things hath done,
in whom His world rejoices;
who from our mother's arms
hath blessed us on our way
with countless gifts of love,
and still is ours today. 🖾

76

The Missing Note

❦

J. Edwin Orr, the revivalist and historian, was with Billy
Graham when the evangelist addressed a meeting in Beverly Hills attended by the notorious gangster Mickey
Cohen. "He expressed some interest in the message," Orr
later wrote, "so several of us talked with him, including
Dr. Graham, but he made no commitment until some
time later when another friend urged him—with Revelation
3:20 as a warrant—to invite Jesus Christ into his life.

"This he professed to do, but his life subsequently
gave no evidence of repentance, 'the mighty change of
mind, heart, and life.' He rebuked our friend, telling him,
'You did not tell me that I would have to give up my
work!' He meant his rackets. 'You did not tell me that I
would have to give up my friends!' He meant his gangster
associates.

"He had heard that so-and-so was a Christian cowboy,

so-and-so was a Christian actress, so-and-so was a Christian senator, and he really thought he could be a Christian gangster.

"The fact is," said Orr, drawing the lesson, "repentance is the missing note in much modern evangelism." ෨

77

The Way It Should Be

❧

I once heard the pastor of Coral Ridge Presbyterian Church in Fort Lauderdale, Dr. James Kennedy, tell of visiting an older gentleman whom he had recently met. Kennedy, seeking to win the man to the Lord, asked him what he thought of Jesus.

"Oh, He's a wonderful man," was the reply. "He was the greatest man who ever lived, the most loving and gracious person who ever walked upon this earth."

Looking intently at the man, Kennedy said, "Let me tell you something I believe will startle you. According to the Scriptures and to the historic Christian faith in all its major branches, Jesus of Nazareth, the carpenter of Galilee *was* and *is* the eternal Creator of the universe, the omnipotent, omniscient, and Almighty God."

Pondering those words, the man began to cry. "I've

been in church all my life, and I've never heard that before," he said. Then he added, "But I've always thought
that's the way it should be." ಜಿ

78

The Investment

❦

Martha Scarborough celebrated Independence Day, July 4, 1870, by giving birth to a son, Lee. When the boy was eight, Martha and her husband George, a part-time Baptist preacher, moved to Texas to raise cattle and share Christ. A dugout shelter served as home, then a log cabin near Clear Fork Creek. George and Martha dreamed of a beautiful house atop a nearby hill. They saved frugally, but times were lean. Years passed before they accumulated enough to proceed with the long-discussed house. Lee, meanwhile, grew into a brawny sixteen-year-old cowboy.

One day, their work behind them, George said to Martha, "Let's go up the hill and select a suitable place for the home. We have saved money for that purpose, so we had as well begin plans to build." Arm in arm, the couple strolled to the grassy crest of the hill behind their cabin. This was a moment long anticipated. At the top of the hill, he said, "Here is the place. This is the most suitable location we can find."

But Martha turned toward him, her eyes filling with tears. "My dear," she said, "I do appreciate your desire to build me a new, comfortable home on this place of beauty, but there is another call for our money which is far greater. Let's live on in the old house and put this money in the head and heart of our boy. I fear that if we use this money to build a home, we shall never be able to send Lee to college. I would rather a thousand times that we should never build this house if we can invest the money in our boy."

George was disappointed, and he said little for several days. Finally one evening past midnight he yielded. The house was never built, but Lee Scarborough left home on January 8, 1888, for Baylor College in Waco, Texas.

He eventually became a powerhouse for Christ, a Southern Baptist leader, a writer, a seminary president, a pastor, an evangelist, and a business leader who built colleges, seminaries, churches, hospitals, and mission stations around the world.

One day in the 1930s, a Bible college student in Florida acquired a book of Lee Scarborough's sermons. Wanting to be a preacher himself, this young man took four of Scarborough's messages and began practicing them, preaching them aloud in the woods to the squirrels and birds. As it happened, he was invited to preach before a human audience shortly afterward on Easter Sunday night, 1937. It was a small, rural church, and the invitation was sudden and unexpected.

Frantically the young man tried to remember Scarborough's four sermons. Getting up to preach, his knees shook and his face glistened with nervous perspiration. He went through all four messages in eight minutes before collapsing back into his seat.

It was Billy Graham's first sermon. ❧

The Bundle in the Barrel

❧

At age thirty-three, A. J. Cronin was a medical doctor in London's West End, and, as he later put it, "I wasn't a bad doctor." But he had trouble finishing projects, and he grew frustrated by his lack of perseverance. He realized it was a character flaw that inhibited everything he did, but he seemed powerless to change himself. He would began studies, hobbies or projects with enthusiasm, then quickly lose energy and discard them for lack of interest.

One day Cronin developed indigestion and at length consulted a colleague who diagnosed gastric ulcers. To Cronin's shock, his friend prescribed six months complete rest in the country on a milk diet.

Cronin retreated to a small farmhouse near the village of Tarbert in the Scottish Highlands. After a week of forced idleness, he felt himself going crazy, bored, reduced to feeding chickens and learning the names of cattle. Looking round for something to do, he recalled that for years he had considered being a writer.

"By heavens!" Cronin said to himself, "This is my opportunity. Gastric ulcer or no gastric ulcer, I will write a novel." Armed with dozens of paper tablets, he closed the door to his cold, clean bedroom and sat down at a small table. There he sat for three hours, trying to think of a way to begin his novel.

Finally he began jotting down words on the page, but he didn't like any of them, and he wadded up sheet after sheet of paper until the waste can overflowed. But out of boredom he kept trying. Three months later, he sent a batch of material to his secretary in London who typed and returned it.

Reading it over, Cronin was horrified. It sounded like such nonsense that he bundled up the papers, threw them in a barrel to be burned, then went walking in the drizzling rain.

Halfway down the shoreline of the lake, he came to old Angus, the farmer, who was patiently and laboriously ditching a patch of heath. As the two men talked, Cronin told the farmer of his decision to abandon writing. The old man was silent a long while before speaking.

"No doubt you're the one that's right, doctor, and I'm the one that's wrong. My father ditched this bog all his days and never made a pasture. I've dug it all my days and I've never made a pasture. But pasture or no pasture, I can not help but dig. For my father knew and I know that if you only dig enough a pasture can be made here."

Cronin, understanding the old man's words, tramped back to the farm. He was drenched and cold, but he collected the soggy bundle from the barrel. He dried the pages at the kitchen oven then flung it onto the table and began to work with a kind of frantic desperation. *I would not be beaten, I would not give in. I wrote harder than ever. At last, toward the end of the third month, I wrote "finis." I had created a book."*

He sent his manuscript to a publisher at random and promptly forgot about it.

On the last day of his stay, Cronin went around the village to say good-bye to those who had befriended him. Entering the post office, he was handed a telegram—an urgent invitation to meet the publisher.

To make a long story short, his novel, *Hatter's Castle*, was chosen by the Book Society, dramatized and serialized, translated into nineteen languages, bought by Hollywood, and went on to sell millions of copies and led to a productive literary career.

"And all because of a timely lesson in the grace of perseverance," he later said.* ﷽

---

*Adapted from A. J. Cronin, "The Turning Point of My Career," in *Getting the Most out of Life,* (Pleasantville, NY: The Reader's Digest Association, Inc., 1946), pp. 1–6.

America's First Missionaries

⋘⋙

Christian parents often worry about sending their sons and daughters to secular colleges and universities, sometimes with good reason. Young people can lose their faith there. But some lose it only to regain it later with added strength.

Adoniram Judson grew up in the 1700s around Boston where his father was a prominent and powerful clergyman. He did well in school and entered Brown University at age 16, graduating valedictorian of his class. While there he became best friends with Jacob Eames. Jacob was a deist and, in practical terms, an atheist. Ridiculing Judson's faith, he challenged him with the writings of Voltaire and the French philosophers. When Adoniram returned home during a school break, he told his parents that he, too, had become an atheist. His mother broke into gentle sobs. His father roared and threatened and pounded the furniture.

Adoniram, twenty-one, migrated to New York City to establish himself as a playwright. But then, hearing tales from the American frontier, he saddled his horse and headed west. One evening, weary from traveling, he stopped at an inn. The proprietor said, "Forgive me, sir, but the only room left—well, it'll be a bit noisy. There's a young fellow next door awfully sick." Adoniram, too tired to care, took the key.

The night became a nightmare. The tramping of feet coming and going. Muffled voices. Painful groans. Chairs scraping against the floor. Adoniram was troubled by it all, and he wondered what his friend Jacob Eames would say about fear, illness, and death.

The next morning while checking out, he asked about the young man in the next room. The proprietor said, "I thought maybe you'd heard. He died, sir, toward morning. Very young. Not more than your age. Went to that Brown University out East." Adoniram stiffened. The man continued, "His name was Jacob Eames."

It was like a slap in the face. The West instantly lost its lure, and Adoniram turned his horse toward home where, to the delight of his praying parents, he gave his life fully to Christ.

Shortly afterward, Adoniram developed a conviction that God wanted him in overseas service. While the British had recently begun sending out missionaries, there had never before been an American missionary. It was understood that missionary service was a virtual death warrant, for most died from disease or martyrdom shortly after their arrival on foreign soil. Judson's family, nevertheless, was supportive.

But what of Adoniram's girlfriend and her family. Following his conversion, he had fallen in love with the most beautiful girl in Bradford, Massachusetts, Ann Hasseltine, daughter of a Congregational deacon. Imagine how her parents felt when reading this letter in which Adoniram asked for Ann's hand in marriage:

I have now to ask whether you can consent to part with your daughter, whether you can consent to her departure to a heathen land, and her subjection to the hardships and suffering of a missionary life? Whether you can consent to her exposure to the dangers of the ocean, to the fatal influence of the southern climate of India, to every kind of want and distress, to degradation, insult, persecution, and perhaps a violent death.

John Hasseltine did consent, and the couple was

married in the Hasseltine home on February 5, 1812. The next day, they were commissioned as America's first foreign missionaries, sailing for Burma on February 18th.

The lesson: The prayers of godly parents follow their children to the university, to the frontier, and to the ends of the earth. J. Sidlow Baxter once pointed out that our loved ones may "spurn our appeals, reject our message, oppose our arguments, despise our persons, but they are helpless against our prayers." ॐ

81

Pit Stop

❧

Successful NASCAR drivers owe as much to their pit crews as to their own skills behind the wheel. One of the finest crew chiefs on the NASCAR circuit is David Smith, who calls the shots in pit row for such drivers as Dale Earnhardt.

In the 1960s, David had plunged headlong into the hippie scene with its trademark consumption of alcohol and drugs. But his father, a new Christian, began witnessing to him.

"Dad," David said, "when I get old like you, I'll get religion."

"What if you were to die today? What if you go to one of these parties tonight and get shot? What if you wreck your car? Where do you think you'll be?"

"Well, I guess I'll be pushing up daisies!"

"No," his father replied, "you've got a soul. That

soul is either going to spend eternity in heaven with the Lord, or in hell."

On his twenty-fifth birthday, his mother gave him a Bible, which he stowed away in a drawer and forget about. But finally . . . *I realized things weren't fun anymore. I was drinking a lot, I was smoking a lot of dope, I was taking a lot of pills, but nothing seemed fun. Something impressed me to get that Bible out of my drawer. I sat down and just started reading. My mother had underlined a bunch of key Scriptures—John 3:16, Romans 3:23, and Romans 6:23: "For the wages of sin is death, but the gift of God is eternal life in Christ Jesus our Lord."*

That evening David read his Bible until far into the night, then found he couldn't sleep. The next morning at 6:30 he called his mom, only to discover she had been so burdened for him that she, too, had spent a sleepless night on her knees.

David turned from his sins to Christ. *And I knew at that moment all the guilt was gone, the burden lifted off my shoulders. In its place a joy and warmness and a complete peace came into my life. Right then.* ❧

82

James Taylor

❧

In the 1700s, a young man named James Taylor proposed marriage to his girlfriend, and a wedding date was set. Neither of them were Christians. James, in fact, detested the itinerant preachers who periodically evangelized his town and often pelted them with rotten tomatoes or eggs.

Shortly before his wedding, one of John Wesley's circuit riders entered town, and James, hearing of it, wanted to disrupt the meeting. But as James listened in the fringes of the crowd, the preacher quoted Joshua 24:15: *But as for me and my house, we will serve the Lord.*

The words stuck James like an arrow.

When the day of his wedding arrived, the verse was still lodged in his thoughts. That morning James retired to the fields to think. He was about to take a wife, to establish a home, but he wasn't serving the Lord. He knelt in the grass and earnestly asked Christ to be his Savior. By the time he finished praying, he was alarmed to discover it was time for the wedding.

Rushing to the chapel, he apologized for being late, and the ceremony proceeded. Then he shocked his bride and guests, by announcing he had become a Christian. He soon began witnessing to his new wife, but she remained resistant. Finally one day James came home so burdened for her that he picked her up and carried her to the bedroom. There with a forceful hand he made her kneel beside him. Soon both were weeping, and there she, too, became a Christian.

Eight generations have since passed, each filled with Christian workers serving the Lord. Included among them is James Taylor's great-grandson, James Hudson Taylor, founder of the China Inland Mission who opened the interior of China to the Gospel of Jesus Christ. ❧

83

All Those Steps

❦

O ne Sunday in Copenhagen, Corrie ten Boom, eighty, spoke from Romans 12:1: *I beseech you therefore, brethren, by the mercies of God, that you present your bodies a living sacrifice, holy, acceptable to God, which is your reasonable service.*

After church two young nurses invited her to their apartment for lunch, and Corrie went with them—only to discover they lived on the tenth floor, and there was no elevator. She didn't think she could mount the stairs, but as the nurses were so eager for her visit she decided to try.

By the fifth floor, Corrie's heart was pounding, her breath coming in gulps, her legs buckling. She collapsed in a chair on the landing thinking she could go no further, and she complained bitterly to the Lord. Looking upward, the stairs seemed to ascend to infinity, and Corrie wondered if she might die en route. "Perhaps I am leaving earth to go to heaven," she thought.

But the Lord seemed to whisper that a special blessing awaited her on the tenth floor, so she bravely pressed on, one nurse in front of her and another following.

Finally reaching the apartment, Corrie found there the parents of one of the girls. She soon discovered that neither parent was a Christian, but both were eager to hear the gospel. Opening her Bible, Corrie carefully explained the plan of salvation. "I have traveled in more than sixty countries and have never found anyone who said they were sorry they had given their hearts to Jesus," she said. "You will not be sorry, either."

That day both prayed for Christ to enter their lives.

On her way down the steps, Corrie said, "Thank you, Lord, for making me walk up all these steps. And next time, Lord, help Corrie ten Boom listen to her own sermon about being willing to go anywhere you tell me to go—even up ten flights of stairs." ❧

84

For His Time

❦

South African pastor Andrew Murray once faced a terrible crisis. Gathering himself into his study, he sat a long while quietly, prayerfully, thoughtfully. His mind flew at last to his Lord Jesus, and picking up his pen, he wrote these words in his journal:

First He brought me here, it is by His will that I am in this strait place: in that fact I will rest.

Next, He will keep me here in His love, and give me grace to behave as His child.

Then, He will make the trial a blessing, teaching me the lessons He intends me to learn, and working in me the grace He means to bestow.

Last, in His good time He can bring me out again—how and when He knows.

Let me say I am here,

(1) By God's appointment.
(2) In His keeping.
(3) Under His training,
(4)For his time. ঌ

85

Angels on the Titanic

❦

C harles Herbert Lightoller was tall, sun-bronzed, and handsome, possessing a deep, pleasant speaking voice. His mother had died during his infancy, his father had abandoned him, and he had run off to sea at the age of thirteen. By 1912, he was a respected seaman for the White Star Line and was assigned to the maiden voyage of the greatest ocean liner ever built, the *Titanic*.

He was just drifting off to sleep on April 14th, when he felt a bump in the ship's forward motion. Hopping from his bunk, he soon learned that the *Titanic* had struck an iceberg. As the horrors of that night unfolded, Lightoller finally found himself standing on the roof of the officer's quarters, the water lapping at his feet, as he helped any and all into lifeboats. Finally there was nothing left for Lightoller to do but jump from the roof into the freezing waters of the North Atlantic.

The shock of the twenty-eight-degree water against his sweating body stunned him, and as he struggled to regain his bearing and swim away from the ship, he was suddenly sucked back and pinned against a ventilation grate at the base of a funnel that went all the way down to boiler room six. He was stuck, drowning, and going down with the ship.

Suddenly Psalm 91:11 came clearly to his mind: *For He shall give His angels charge over you, To keep you in all your ways* . . .

At that very moment, a blast of hot air exploded from the belly of the ship, shooting Lightoller like a missile to the surface of the ocean. At length, he managed to grab a piece of rope attached to the side of an overturned lifeboat and float along with it until he pulled himself on top of the upside-down boat.

He turned and watched the last moments of the *Titanic*. Her stern swung up in the air until the ship was in "an absolutely perpendicular position." Then she slowly sank down into the water, with only a small gulp as her stern disappeared beneath the waves.

There were about thirty men atop the lifeboat and together they recited the Lord's Prayer, then Lightoller took command of the boat and guided them to safety.

The British "Prince of Preachers," Charles Spurgeon, once told his congregation: *I do not know how to explain it; I can not tell how it is; but I believe angels have a great deal to do with the business of this world.*

You are not alone. ॐ

86

The Man
Behind Quaker Oats

◆§◈§◆

When Henry Crowell was nine his father died from tuberculosis, and when he was seventeen Henry himself contracted the disease. He appeared to be dying as he attended D.L. Moody's evangelistic campaign in Cleveland, Ohio. He listened carefully as Moody, quoting his friend Henry Varley, thundered: "The world has yet to see what God can do through a man fully dedicated to him."

Crowell determined to be God's man. *Moody's words were the words of the Lord to me. . . . To be sure, I would never preach like Moody. But I could make money and support the labors of men like Moody. I resolved, "Oh God, if you preserve my life and allow me to make money to be used in your service, I will keep my name out of it so you will have the glory."*

Shortly thereafter Henry found Job 5:19: "He shall deliver you in six troubles, Yes, in seven no evil shall touch you." The Lord seemed to assure him of healing through that verse.

Henry grew stronger and began honing his business instincts, shrewdly investing his family's wealth. He started companies, purchased properties, and introduced innovations to the marketplace. When a mill owned by nearby Quakers became available, Henry purchased it and began dreaming of modern cereal products for American homes. Thus Quaker Oats Company was born.

The money rolled in—and it rolled out. Henry consistently gave 65 to 70 percent of his income to Christian causes. Millions of dollars flowed to churches, schools, and missions. He worked tirelessly for the new, fledgling Moody Bible Institute of Chicago. Under his vision, MBI escaped financial ruin and became a powerful training center. He helped start Moody Press, Moody Magazine, and Moody radio ministries, frequently reminding his co-laborers, "Take your time, be sure to take your time. Be sure to find the will of God. When folks do not agree with you, let them talk. Be quiet while they talk. When they've talked themselves out, they'll ask what you think should be done. Tell them, they'll do it."

In his last address to graduating seniors at Moody Bible Institute, Crowell warned, "The more competent you are, the stronger will be the temptation to yield to the power of accumulating activities. The temptation will be to take time for these activities that belongs to your devotions. . . . Something must be given up. Reluctantly and slowly you lessen the time set aside for devotions—then comes the curtailment of power. I plead with you, refuse to lessen the devotional period, no matter how severe the pressure.

After his death, his family found a card on his desk. It had been written forty years before, and he had carried it in his pocket through the passing decades. On it, he had scribbled his soul's philosophy: *If my life can be always lived so as to please Him, I'll be supremely happy.* &

87

Yet Will I Trust Him

❧⟨§⟩❧

Shortly after the death of their daughter Robin, Roy Rogers and Dale Evans met a pale little boy who stuck out his hand and said, "Howdy, pahtnah!" He had been abandoned in a Kentucky motel, and was physically and mentally disabled.

Roy and Dale adopted him, calling him Sandy in honor of his hair. He was bright-eyed and good-natured. He had trouble riding tricycles, he often fell, and he proved emotionally fragile. But they gave him medical attention, good food, and lots of love. During a Billy Graham Crusade, Sandy made a decision for Christ and grew quickly in the Lord.

As Sandy grew older, Roy and Dale enrolled him in military school and he loved it. At seventeen, he enlisted in the army "to prove myself." Sandy worked hard and won respect. He was sent to Germany, then volunteered for Vietnam. "Put your faith in the Lord," he wrote home, "because (as I have found out) He's always around when you need Him. All He asks in return is your devotion."

Then one day Dale Evans, returning from a trip, was met at the airport. "It's Sandy, Mom. He's dead." The news hit her hard, and it grew worse. Sandy had returned from 26 days of maneuvers, dog tired. His buddies had taken him out for the night, needling him to "prove you're a man." Sandy, who couldn't tolerate alcohol, had given in. They fed him hard liquor until he collapsed. He was found the next morning dead in his bunk.

Dale Evans survived the sorrow only by drawing strength from Scripture, particularly from Job 13:15. "Tragedy in a Christian's life is a refiner," she wrote. "God has not promised an easy way, but peace at the center of the hard way. The clouds of sorrow have been heavy, but I have reached the point of no return in my Christian experience, and with Job I can cry, 'Though He slay me, yet will I trust Him.'"

"When you can't trace His hand," Charles Spurgeon once said, "you can trust His heart." ॐ

256 ॐ

88

"What If We Make Mistakes?"

&cscs&

Several years ago I was invited to a political briefing in Washington. Among our speakers was the venerable Senator Jennings Randolph of West Virginia who had first been elected to Congress in 1933. He was the only remaining member of the U.S. Senate or House of Representatives who had been elected in the great landslide of votes that had elevated Franklin D. Roosevelt to the presidency during the Great Depression. At the time of our meeting, Sen. Randolph was aged, but still keen of mind.

We had many questions for him, and during the course of our interview, he told us this story. Just after Roosevelt's inauguration in 1933, Randolph was called to the White House. Having only recently arrived in Washington, he was surprised by the call and entered the White

House wide-eyed. The young congressman couldn't believe he had been included, as young and inexperienced as he was. But Roosevelt had his eye on Jennings Randolph.

There in the president's private quarters sat FDR. The lights were low, and a fire was roaring in the fireplace. About a dozen or so leaders of Congress had come at FDR's request. Randolph recognized their faces, but he was intimidated and didn't say much that night. He just sat in awe as Franklin Roosevelt began to speak. Roosevelt told the congressional leaders what he had in mind, and how quickly he wanted to move during the first one hundred days of his administration.

The President said he intended to declare a bank holiday, a positive-sounding phrase that really meant closing all the nation's banks indefinitely until bankers and the government could regain control of the situation. He wanted to send Congress a record number of bills to be acted upon quickly and furiously, including the creation of the Civilian Conservation Corps, the Tennessee Valley Authority, and the Federal Emergency Relief Administration.

He went on and on, speaking confidently, but in such low tones that Randolph had to strain to hear him. But when FDR was finished, the group sat in stunned silence, unable to grasp the extent of the President's vision. Finally one of the senators said, "Mr. President, if we move that quickly aren't you afraid we'll make mistakes?"

Jennings Randolph never forgot the President's reply.

Looking the questioner in the eye, FDR said, "Senator, if we *don't* move that quickly, we may lose the opportunity of even making mistakes." ❧

The Woman Who Regretted Her Own Holiday

❧

Mother's Day, in one form or another, has been around a long time. In ancient Greece, a celebration honoring mothers occurred every spring.

In the Middle Ages, a custom called *Mothering Sunday* began when children, who often left home early to learn a trade or become apprentices, would be released from work every year on the forth Sunday of Lent to attend church with their families. As they returned home, they often took cakes or little gifts to their mothers. This was termed "going a-mothering." To this day, Mother's Day in the United Kingdom is celebrated on the fourth Sunday of Lent.

It was in 1872 that Julia Ward Howe (author of *The Battle Hymn of the Republic*) suggested the idea of Mother's Day in the United States.

The cause was taken up by Anna Jarvis, daughter of a Methodist pastor. Jarvis felt the scars of the Civil War could be healed by mothers—and by honoring mothers. She died in 1905 before her dream of establishing a holiday could be fulfilled. But her daughter, also named Anna Jarvis, took up the crusade.

Anna had been deeply influenced by her mother, and she often recalled hearing her mother say that she hoped someone would one day establish a memorial for all mothers, living and dead.

Anna had been particularly touched at age twelve while listening to her mother teach a Sunday School class on the subject "Mothers in the Bible." Mrs. Jarvis closed the lesson with a prayer to this effect: *I hope and pray that someone, sometime, will found a memorial mother's day. There are many days for men, but none for mothers.*

Anna never forgot that moment, and at their mother's graveside service, Anna's brother Claude heard her say ". . . by the grace of God, you shall have that Mother's Day."

Anna thus began a campaign to establish a national

Mother's Day. She and her supporters began to write a constant stream of letters to ministers, businessmen, politicians and newspaper editors. She spent a fortune trying to attract attention to her idea, and took every opportunity to give speeches, send telegrams, or write articles promoting her cause.

On the second anniversary of her mother's death, May 12, 1907, Anna led a small tribute to her mother at Andrews Methodist Episcopal Church in Gafton, West Virginia. She donated five hundred white carnations, her mother's favorite flower, to be worn by everyone in attendance. On this first Mother's Day service, the pastor used the text, "Woman, behold thy son; Son, behold thy mother" (John 19:26). That same day a special service was held at the Wannamaker Auditorium in Philadelphia, which could seat no more than a third of the fifteen thousand people who showed up.

After that, things began to take off. Various states jumped the bandwagon, officially proclaiming a Mother's Day each year; and in 1914, President Woodrow Wilson officially established Mother's Day as a national holiday to be held on the second Sunday of May.

But having succeeded at last, Anna Jarvis soon became embittered by the commercialization of her holiday and turned against it, actually filing a lawsuit to stop a 1923 Mother's Day festival. She was even arrested for disturbing the peace at a mother's convention where women sold white carnations.

"This is not what I intended," Jarvis growled. "I wanted it to be a day of sentiment, not profit!"

"A printed card means nothing except that you are too lazy to write to the woman who has done more for you than anyone in the world," she said on another occasion. "And candy! You take a box to Mother—and then eat most of it yourself. A pretty sentiment."

Shortly before her death in 1948 Anna Jarvis, living in a nursing home, received Mother's Day cards from all around the world. But she told a reporter she was sorry she had ever started the whole thing.

We aren't, for it gives us an annual opportunity to obey one of Scripture's sweetest commandments— "Honor thy . . . mother" (Exodus 20:12).

Proverbs 31:30–31 says: "Charm is deceitful and beauty is passing, But a woman who fears the LORD, she shall be praised. Give her of the fruit of her hands, And let her own works praise her in the gates." ﷼

│   **90**   │
└─────────────┘

Practicing the Presence of God

❧❦❧

After twenty-three years in the pastorate, I'm seldom shocked. But I was a little surprised recently with Joey, a typical teen, mixed up, battling hormones, confused, experimenting. The other day he sauntered into my office, slouched in the chair, and told me he'd found a book that had really gotten hold of him. Pulling a tattered paperback from his coat pocket, he handed it to me.

It was over three hundred years old—*The Practice of the Presence of God*—written in the seventeenth century by a Parisian cook named Nicholas Herman (pronounced är-män), otherwise known as Brother Lawrence.

Who is this outdated mystic who can still reach teenage boys?

Nicholas was born in Lorraine, France, in 1605, but

264 ❦ ———————————————————————————

little is known of his early life. He reached his own teen years at the onset of the Thirty Years' War, during which he fought for the French army, was seriously wounded, and was lame for the rest of his life. Converted at age 18, he went to work as a footman for a local official in the treasury.

Years passed, and at age fifty Nicholas joined a Carmelite monastery in Paris where he was dubbed Brother Lawrence and assigned to the kitchen, a task that struck him as insulting and humbling. For the next several years, he went about his chores, miserable but dutifully, until gradually recognizing his unhealthy attitude.

He began reminding himself frequently that God's presence continually hovered about him, and his disposition changed. Even the most menial tasks, Lawrence realized, if undertaken for God's glory, are holy; and wherever the Christian stands—even in a hot, thankless kitchen—is holy ground, for the Lord is there, too.

Many more years passed, and Brother Lawrence's countenance and demeanor gradually changed until others began asking him a reason for his radiance. He was sought out and his advice valued. Christian leaders listened to him, and one man was particularly impressed—the Abbot of Beaufort.

The two met four times and exchanged fifteen letters to discuss Brother Lawrence's walk with the Lord. The Abbot made notes of the conversations and preserved the letters, compiling them into the book known today as *The Practice of the Presence of God.* It was published in the mid-1600s, shortly after Lawrence's death.

One of the best things about this book is its brevity. My edition is only thirty-five pages, making it inexpensive, and it can be re-read frequently and absorbed. It begins in a simple, pedestrian manner: *The first time I saw Brother Lawrence was upon the 3rd day of August, 1666. He told me that God had done him a singular favor in his conversion at age eighteen. . . .*

The Abbot went on to quote Brother Lawrence as saying, *we should establish ourselves in a sense of God's presence by continually conversing with Him.* Lawrence admitted that practicing the presence of God requires applying ourselves to it with some diligence at first, but in due time *His love inwardly excites us to it without any difficulty.* The Christian life is *a continual conversation with Him. . . . We need only to recognize God intimately present with us.*

The Abbot wrote, *It was observed that in the great hurry of business in the kitchen he still preserved his recollection and heavenly-mindedness. He was never hasty nor loitering, but did each thing in its season, with an even, uninterrupted composure and tranquility of spirit.*

The time of business, said the Brother, *does not with me differ from the time of prayer, and in the noise and clatter of my kitchen, while several persons are at the same time calling for different things, I possess God in as great tranquility as if I were upon my knees at the blessed sacrament.*

Among Brother Lawrence's quotes:

- *Think often on God, by day, by night, in your business, and even in your diversions. He is always near you and with you; leave Him not alone. You would think it rude to leave a friend alone who came to visit you; why, then, must God be neglected?*
- *When we are faithful to keep ourselves in His holy presence and set Him always before us, this not only hinders our offending Him and doing anything that may displease Him . . . but it also begets in us a holy freedom, and, if I may so speak, a familiarity with God, wherewith we ask, and that successfully, the graces we stand in need of.*
- *The presence of God (is) a subject which, in my opinion, contains the whole spiritual life; and it seems to me that whoever duly practices it will soon become spiritual.*

▪ *Were I a preacher, I should, above all other things, preach the practice of the presence of God.*

When Brother Lawrence lay on his deathbed, rapidly losing physical strength, he said to those around him "I am not dying. I am just doing what I have been doing for the past forty years, and doing what I expect to be doing for all eternity!"

"What is that?" they asked.

"I am worshipping the God I love!" ❧

91

"Hey, Were You Guys Praying?"

∽§§∾

Charles Colson, former special assistant to President Richard Nixon, went to prison for his role in the Watergate scandal and was converted to Christ through reading C. S. Lewis' *Mere Christianity.*

He wrote of his conversion in *Born Again,* a book that was launched with a backbreaking tour that ended up in California. Arriving late at his hotel, he and his friend Fred Denne, went to the coffee shop for a snack. The room had a Spanish motif—red tile on the floor, wrought iron tables and chairs. A waitress in a pink uniform waited on them. The men noticed she looked like a young starlet, blondish hair and pleasant-faced.

"Two cheese omelets, one milk and one iced tea," said Fred.

After she left, the two men reviewed the next day's schedule a few minutes, then decided to ask the Lord's blessings on their anticipated meal. They bowed their heads, and, as blessings go, it was fairly long. When they raised their heads, the waitress was standing nearby, omelets in hand.

"Hey," she said loudly, "were you guys praying?" Everyone in the small room turned to look at them.

"Yes, we were," said Colson.

"Hey, that's neat," said the waitress. "I've never seen anybody do that in here before. Are you preachers?"

They said no, but she persisted in asking questions. Then she said, "I'm a Christian. At least I was once."

"What happened?" the men asked.

"I accepted Jesus as my Savior at a rally when I was a teenager. Then I went to live in Hawaii. Well, I just lost interest, I guess. Forgot about it."

"I don't think you lost it," Colson said gently. "You just put it aside for a while."

The waitress seemed thoughtful. "It's funny, but the moment I saw you guys praying I felt excited all over again."

They talked to her at some length about renewing her commitment to the Lord. They discussed the story of prodigal son and talked to her about the Lord's love and forgiveness. Later during their stay at the hotel, they saw her again. "Hey, you guys," she shouted. She told them she had already called a Christian friend and was joining a Bible study the next day. "And I'm going to find a church, too. I've come back."

"Until that night," Colson later said, "I had felt awkward at times praying over meals in crowded restaurants. Never again."* ❧

---

*Adapted from Charles W. Colson, *Life Sentence* (Minneapolis: World Wide, 1979, pp. 105–106.

92

Going to Church in Bad Weather

❦

Sunday night, February 13, 1889, was bitterly cold. The thermometer registered twenty-two below zero, and most people huddled by their fires trying to stay alive. But Eugene Sallee, a brilliant student at Georgetown College in Kentucky, suggested to his roommate that they attend evening worship. "Let's go to church tonight," he said. "The pastor will not have many present."

He was right. The congregation consisted of Sallee, his roommate, and a small handful that braved the elements. Despite the small number, Pastor Z. T. Cody did his best, preaching on the subject, "Moses' Wise Choice," from Hebrews 11:24–25: *By faith Moses, when he became of age, refused to be called the son of Pharaoh's daughter, choosing rather to suffer affliction with the people of God than to enjoy the passing pleasures of sin.*

For some reason, every sentence hit young Eugene like the blow of a hammer. Cody described how Moses, the darling of Pharaoh's household, had been trained in all the wisdom of Egypt. Wealth and position were his. But when God called him, he obeyed, choosing "rather to suffer affliction with the people of God than to enjoy the passing pleasures of sin."

Until that night Sallee had planned for a career in law, but Dr. Cody's sermon perturbed him as he trudged through the dangerous cold back to his room. He wondered if the Lord was calling him to ministry. To missions? He pushed the thoughts aside and, graduating from Georgetown, he applied to Columbia Law School in New York.

Sallee spent the summer following his graduation in Missouri, riding horseback across the countryside selling aluminum ware. But Cody's sermon from Hebrews 11 wouldn't release its grip on his soul. Finally one day as he rode along, Eugene came to a quiet stream. Tethering his horse to a tree, he wandered into the dense woods, found a place to pray, and there surrendered his life to fulltime Christian service.

In time, the Lord led him to China where he devoted twenty-seven remarkable years in evangelization and church-planting. "For this cause came I into the world," he once said, "and to this end I was born, to preach the gospel in China."

. . . all of which reminds me of the little poem Vance Havner quoted about his father, a godly man who never used bad weather as an excuse for staying away from church:

> *Whether the weather be good*
> *Or whether the weather be hot,*
> *Whether the weather be cold*
> *Or whether the weather be not,*
> *Whatever the weather, he weathered the weather,*
> *Whether he liked it or not.* ঽ

93

The Tongue Screw

❧§❧

Travel brochures of the Netherlands tell of windmills, dikes, and boys named Hans with their silver skates. But the years 1531 to 1578 were not so peaceful. Hundreds of Protestants were slaughtered, including another young man named Hans.

Hans Bret supported his widowed mother by working in a bakery in Antwerp. The two belonged to a Protestant group there, and in his spare time Hans studied the Bible and taught new converts in the church, preparing them for baptism. One evening a knock sounded on the bakery door. Hans opened it to find a delegation of officers. The house was surrounded and Hans was arrested. For the next several months, authorities alternately questioned and tortured him. From his dark isolation hole, Hans managed to smuggle letters to his mother.

From Him alone we expect our strength to withstand these cruel wolves, so that they have no power over our souls. They are really more cruel than wolves—they are not satisfied with our bodies, tearing at them; but they seek to devour and kill our souls.

Hans' treatment worsened, and, when intense torture failed to break his spirit, he was sentenced to the stake. Early on Saturday, January 4, 1577, the executioner came to Hans' cell and ordered him to stick out his tongue. Over it he clamped an iron tongue screw, twisting it tightly with a vice grip. Then he seared the end of Hans' tongue with a red-hot iron so that the tongue would swell and couldn't slip out of the clamp. The officials didn't want Hans preaching at his execution. The young man was taken by wagon to the marketplace, secured to a post with winding chains, and burned alive.

In the crowd, another Hans watched in horror—Hans de Ries, Bret's pastor and friend. After the ashes cooled, he sifted through them and retrieved a keepsake—the tongue screw that had fallen from Bret's consumed body. Shortly after, Hans de Ries married Hans Bret's mother, and the tongue screw became a symbol of faithfulness that has passed from generation to generation.

We must retain and revere such stories, for they are the threads from which our heritage is spun, by which our faith has been passed to us strand by strand. They are men and women of whom the world is not worthy. Our martyred forefathers, we read in Revelation 12:11, have prevailed over Satan, overcoming him by the blood of the Lamb and by the word of their testimony, and they did not love their lives so much as to shrink from death.

94

Broken and Spilled Out

⚜

It was a terrible fall, and it sickened those who saw it. John Pounds, a tall, muscular teen laborer at the docks of Portsmouth, England, slipped and plunged from the top of a ship's mast, pitching headfirst into the bowels of the vessel. When fellow workers reached him, he was nothing but a mass of broken bones. For two years he lay in bed as his bones healed crookedly. His pain never ceased. Out of boredom, he began to read the Bible.

At length, John crawled from bed hoping to find something he could do with his life. A shoemaker hired him, and day after day, John sat at his cobbler's bench, a Bible open on his lap. Soon he was born again.

John ultimately gathered enough money to purchase his own little shoeshop, and one day he developed a pair of surgical boots for his crippled nephew Johnny, whom he had taken in. Soon John was making corrective shoes for other children, and his little cobbler's shop became a miniature children's hospital.

As John's burden for children grew, he began receiving homeless ones, feeding them, teaching them to read, and telling them about the Lord. His shop became known as "The Ragged School," and John would limp around the waterfront, food in his pockets, looking for more children to tend.

During his lifetime, John Pounds rescued 500 children from despair and led every one of them to Christ. Moreover, his work became so famous that a "Ragged School Movement" swept England, and a series of laws were passed to establish schools for poor children in John's honor. Boy's homes, girl's homes, day schools, and evening schools were started, along with Bible classes in which thousands heard the gospel.

When John collapsed and died on New Year's Day, 1839 while tending to a boy's ulcerated foot, he was buried in a churchyard on High Street. All England mourned, and a monument was erected over his grave with this quotation from Luke 14:14: "Thou shalt be blessed, for they could not recompense thee" (KJV). ❧

95

God's Handwriting

ᨑᨑᨑ

Missionaries Dick and Margaret Hillis found themselves caught in China during the Japanese invasion. The couple lived with their two children in the inland town of Shenkiu. The village was tense with fear, for every day brought terrifying reports of the Japanese advance. At the worst possible time, Dick developed appendicitis, and he knew his life depended on making the long journey by rickshaw to the hospital. On January 15, 1941, with deep foreboding, Margaret watched him leave.

Soon the Chinese colonel came with news. The enemy was near and townspeople must evacuate. Margaret shivered, knowing that one-year-old Johnny and two-month-old Margaret Anne would never survive as refugees. So she stayed put. Early next morning she tore the page from the wall calendar and read the new day's Scripture. It was Psalm 56:3—*What time I am afraid, I will trust in thee.**

The town emptied during the day, and the next morning Margaret arose, feeling abandoned. The new verse on the calendar was Psalm 9:10—*Thou, Lord, hast not forsaken them that seek thee.*

The next morning she arose to distant sounds of gunfire and worried about food for her children. The calendar verse was Genesis 50:21—*I will nourish you and your little ones.* An old woman suddenly popped in with a pail of steaming goat's milk, and another straggler arrived with a basket of eggs.

Through the day, sounds of warfare grew louder, and during the night Margaret prayed for deliverance. The next morning she tore the page from the calendar to read Psalm 56:9—*When I cry unto Thee, then shall my enemies turn back.* The battle was looming closer, and Margaret didn't go to bed that night. Invasion seemed imminent. But the next morning, all was quiet. Suddenly, villagers began returning to their homes, and the colonel knocked on her door. For some reason, he told her, the Japanese had withdrawn their troops. No one could understand it, but the danger had passed. They were safe.

_____

*Scriptures from KJV.

   Margaret glanced at her wall calendar and felt she had been reading the handwriting of God. ❧

96

Apostle of Bleeding Feet

❧❦❧

The Indian Christian Sundar Singh once ventured into the forbidden land of Nepal on the borders of Tibet to preach Jesus. In a village there, as he distributed copies of Mark's Gospel, one of his listeners ripped the Gospel apart and hurried to notify town officials. Sundar was promptly thrown into jail, but he used the time to witness to his fellow prisoners.

When the jailer forbade him from evangelizing, Sundar, sounding much like Peter, replied, "I must obey my Master and preach His gospel, regardless of threats and sufferings."

The jailer ordered the prisoners not to listen, but they replied, "This man tells us how we can become better, which is what we need."

Sundar was taken from the cell to a filthy cattle shed. The jailer stripped off his clothing, tied him down hand

and foot, and threw upon him a swarm of leeches that had been collected from the jungle. The loathsome creatures latched onto his body and began sucking his blood. *But, I lifted up my heart to God in prayer, and He sent such heavenly peace into my soul that I soon began to sing His praises.*

After he had grown weak from loss of blood, the authorities released him and returned his clothes. Sundar was soon seen again in the center of town, preaching the gospel and telling the people, *It is a joy to suffer for my Savior. In bearing my cross, I hope to direct men to His cross with its offer of peace and pardon. In the cross of Christ alone I will ever glory.*

Who was this unusual man who, during his lifetime, was one of the world's most admired Christian heroes? Sundar Singh was born into a wealthy family in India in 1889. His mother trained him from birth to become a Sikh holy man, and by age seven he could quote by heart vast portions of Hindu holy books. Seeing his intelligence, his mother eventually sent him to a Presbyterian school for a one-year's course in English. There Sundar, forced to read the New Testament, rebelled, his hot-blooded heart raging against his missionary teachers.

Being tall, good-looking, and muscular, he quickly

became the leader of the anti-Christian students, on one ocasion burning a Bible page by page before them.

But Sundar's white-hot emotions couldn't absorb the tragic death of his mother, and he found himself at age fifteen overcome with despair. On Sunday night, December 17, 1904, he went to bed planning to commit suicide before breakfast. He rose according to plan at three a.m., took a ceremonial cold bath in keeping with Hindu custom, and prepared to cast himself in front of the five a.m. express train speeding by his house.

But as Sundar prayed, a light suddenly illumed the room, shining so brightly that he thought the house ablaze. A strong, serene figure seemed to appear in a vaporous white cloud and in perfect Hindustani spoke these words: "Why do you persecute me? Remember that I gave My life for you upon the cross."

Sundar was instantly converted to Christ. When he later shared the news with his family, they were appalled, and failing to dissuade him, they tried to poison him. But Sundar, not to be denied, was baptized on his sixteenth birthday. He sought theological training, and soon put on the yellow robe and turban of a sadhu, a wandering holy man, to go forth preaching the gospel.

Through the mountain passes and over the rugged hills of northern India he journeyed, braving hardship and persecution. He was imprisoned. He was stoned. He was tortured. He was thrown into wells, naked, to die. His travels were so rigorous that he was called the "Apostle of the Bleeding Feet."

Yet his dark, shining eyes, full beard, and graceful poise reminded people of the Savior, and many believed he looked expressly like Jesus. Great crowds gathered to hear him, and his fame spread throughout the Orient, then around the world. In the years that followed, he preached in some of the greatest pulpits of Asia, Europe, and America. Biographies of him were written and stories about him printed. His face was known everywhere.

Then he disappeared. Being a missionary at heart, Sandu longed to take the gospel into the mysterious and forbidden land of Tibet. In April, 1929, spurning the advice of friends, he set out into the Himalayan foothills, heading upward and inward, disappearing from sight. He was never seen again.

"It is a joy," he once said, "to suffer for my Savior. In bearing *my* cross, I hope to direct men to *His* cross. It was *that* cross that lifted me out of despair into the peace of God and in the cross of Christ alone I will ever glory." ❧

97

Faith Under Fire

❦

On several occasions near the end of the Cold War, our church had the privilege of hearing Joseph Tson, the Baptist pastor and evangelical dissident who was expelled from Communist Romania for his testimony and Christian witness. On one occasion, he told us how Christian students at Romania's universities identified each other during the Communist regime. Since it was illegal and dangerous to be a believer, it was difficult for Christian students to locate and fellowship with each other. But they learned to walk around the campus whistling the tunes to hymns. The Communists, who didn't know the hymns, paid no attention, but Christian students recognized the melodies. In this way they were able to meet their brothers and sisters in Christ.

Tson also told of being frequently summoned before

government officers who used every tactic to break his faith in Christ.

Once, being interrogated at Ploiesti, an officer threatened to kill him.

"Sir," replied Tson, "let me explain how I see this issue. Your supreme weapon is killing. My supreme weapon is dying."

When the officer looked skeptical, Tson explained, "Here is how it works. You know that my sermons on tape have spread all over the country. If you kill me, those sermons will be sprinkled with my blood. Everyone will know I died for my preaching. And everyone who has a tape will pick it up and say, 'I'd better listen again to what this man preached, because he really meant it; he sealed it with his life.'

"So, sir, my sermons will speak ten times louder than before. I will actually rejoice in this supreme victory if you kill me."

The officer sent Tson home. ❧

98

James Gilmore's Long Distance Wife

❧

When James Gilmore sailed for China in 1870, he was young, strong, and in need of a wife. He plunged into re-opening the London Missionary Society's work in Mongolia, but with no one to lean on. "Companions I can scarcely hope to meet," he wrote, "and the feeling of being alone comes over me." As labors increased, so did loneliness. "Today I felt a good deal like Elijah in the wilderness," he told his journal. "He prayed that he might die . . . I felt drawn towards suicide. Two missionaries should always go together. Oh! the intense loneliness. . . ."

The pain deepened when his proposal to a Scotch girl was rejected, but James rallied his faith and had a talk with the Lord about his problem. He later wrote, "I then put myself and the direction of this affair—I mean the finding of a wife—into God's hands, asking Him to look me out one, a good one, too."

In 1873, Gilmore, needing a break from his work, visited friends in Peking, a Mr. and Mrs. Meech. On the piano, he saw a picture of Mrs. Meech's sister, Emily Prankard, and James asked about her. As his hostess described Emily, James found himself falling in love. He gazed at her picture, saw some of her letters, and asked more and more questions.

Early next year, James wrote to Emily, proposing marriage in his first letter. By the same mail he informed his parents in Scotland: "I have written and proposed to a girl in England. It is true I have never seen her, and I know very little about her, but I have put the whole matter into the hands of God, asking Him, if it be best, to bring her, if it be not best, to keep her away, and He can manage the whole thing well."

Receiving Gilmore's letter, Emily took it at once to the throne of grace. Later Gilmore recalled, "The first letter I wrote her was to propose, and the first letter she wrote me was to accept." By autumn, Emily was in China, arriving on November 29, 1874. A week later, they were married. Gilmore acquired both wife and colleague, and they labored faithfully side by side for years, reaching northern China for Christ.

When the Lord is our Shepherd, He sends food with the ravens, manna from heaven, water from the rocks, and life from the tombs. He sets the solitary in families, and those who seek first the Kingdom of God and His righteousness find all genuine needs of life met, sometimes in ways unusual. ॐ

99

Vietnam

❧❦❧

His nightmares began each day when he awoke.

James Stegalls was nineteen. He was in Vietnam. Though he carried a small Gideon New Testament in his shirt pocket, he couldn't bring himself to read it. His buddies were cut down around him, terror was building within him, and God seemed far away. His twentieth birthday passed, then his twenty-first. At last, he felt he couldn't go on.

On February 26, 1968, he prayed for it all to end, and his heart told him he would die before dusk. Sure enough, his base came under attack that day, and Jim heard a rocket coming straight toward him. Three seconds to live, he told himself, then two, then . . .

A friend shoved him into a grease pit, and he waited for the rocket to explode, but there was only a surreal silence. The fuse malfunctioned.

For five hours James knelt in that pit, and finally his quivering hand reached into his shirt pocket and took out his Testament. Beginning with Matthew, he continued through the first eighteen chapters.

"When I read Matthew 18:19–20," he said, "I somehow knew things would be all right."

Long after Jim returned home, as he visited his wife's grandmother, Mrs. Harris, she told him a night years before when she had awakened in terror. Knowing Jim was in Vietnam, she had sensed he was in trouble. She began praying for God to spare his life. Unable to kneel because of arthritis, she lay prone on the floor, praying and reading her Bible all night.

Just before dawn she read Matthew 18:19–20: *If two of you agree down here on earth concerning anything you ask, my Father in heaven will do it for you. For where two or three gather together because they are mine, I am there among them.*

She immediately called her Sunday School teacher who got out of bed and went to Mrs. Harris' house where together they claimed the Lord's promise as they prayed for Jim until reassured by God's peace.

Having told Jim the story, Mrs. Harris opened

her Bible to show him where she had marked the passage.

In the margin were the words: *Jim, February 26, 1968.* * ॐ

---

*Adapted from Jim L. Stegall, "Hardly a Coincidence" in *Changed Lives: USA Testimonies*.

100

New Perspective

❧❦❧

Sadie Smithson grew up in Johnson Falls, West Virginia. Her father kept a livery stable; Sadie herself contributed to the family income by sewing. The family floated just above the poverty level. But Sadie craved respect. She wanted to mingle with the upper crust of Johnson Falls, and she had a plan for doing it. Her secret ambition was to join the Laurel Literary Society, an organization that represented all that was socially prestigious in her town. After high school graduation, she applied for admission into the Laurel Literary Society.

Nothing doing. She was rejected.

Well, she thought, perhaps they'll think better of me if I tour Europe. Few in Johnson Falls had ever been abroad. So she saved her money, daydreaming of the soft-gloved hands clapping after she had read her paper on "My Trip to Europe."

After many years, she had saved enough money. Finally she took her long-planned trip abroad, traveling with a professor and his wife, only to be caught in the opening shots of World War I. Sadie, in Belgium at the time, managed to get a ride to Paris; but the driver lost his way, and they suddenly found themselves crossing a battlefield.

Right beside the car lay one young soldier, badly wounded. He looked into Sadie's eyes and moaned, "Water, for God's sake!" Sadie immediately jumped out of the car with her drinking cup and made her way to a nearby spring. Then another dying soldier wanted a drink. Sadie refused to leave those boys, and finally the car drove off without her. All night long, she ran back and forth to the spring with her little cup, carrying water to injured men. She tore her skirt into bandages. She scribbled notes and messages for loved ones at home. And as she worked with each wounded man, she offered a prayer: "The Lord bless you and keep you and make His face to shine upon you."

It was a night of horror, of darkness, and of moaning, dying men. Finally the darkness gave way to the dawn, and with it an ambulance and young doctor. He was astonished to find a poor girl from West Virginia amid all the blood and carnage of war. "Who are you?" he asked, "And what in thunder are you doing here?"

"I'm Sadie Smithson," she said, "And I've been holding hell back all night."

"Well!" said the young doctor quietly, "well, Miss Sadie Smithson, I'm glad you held some of it back, for everybody else in the world was letting it loose last night."

As she was returning to America, she told her story to a fellow passenger on the ship. "I've never been married—never known what it was to have children—but that night all those men were my children, even the biggest and roughest of them, and I believe I could have died for any one of them."

"Well," said the friend, "the Laurel Literary Society will be glad enough to have you belong to it now."

"No," Sadie Smithson replied, "I've been face to face with war and death and hell and God. Now little things like the Laurel Literary Society don't matter to me anymore."

"What does matter?" asked the friend.

"Nothing," Sadie said. "Nothing but God and love—and doing what I can do for those He sends me to."

Jesus Christ came in the darkness of night to a dying race of humanity. He loved us and gave Himself for us. When we receive Him, our perspective is permanently altered and so is our attitude. The trivial and the important change places.

_____

*Adapted from a story in William L. Stidger, *There Are Sermons in Stories* (New York: Abingdon, mvmxlii), pp. 11–13.

101

The Bananas

❧

Darlene Deiblier Rose, in her fascinating autobiography titled *Evidence Not Seen,* tells of her career as a missionary in the Asian Pacific at the outset of World War II. She and her husband were captured by the Japanese and interred in concentration camps. Her husband perished, and in her book, Darlene tells horrific stories of her own suffering and of how God sustained her.

The food she was given was loathsome, and often she found worms and insects swimming around in the miserable soup she was given to eat. At first, she was so repulsed she couldn't eat it, but she gradually learned that it was necessary for her survival to crush the worms and insects in her fingers and eat them with her soup.

She developed severe dysentery and diarrhea, and her condition became very debilitating and embarrassing to her. She was given Epsom salts and quinine, but to no avail. Finally she just brought her condition to the Lord. "Lord," she simply prayed, "I'm being constantly reinfected by these flies, so if it please You, heal me."

The Lord gave her a sense of faith about this matter, so that when later in the day the guard brought her the daily doses of Epsom salts and quinine, she refused to take them. All symptoms left her, not only of dysentery, but of malaria and beriberi, from which she had also suffered. She was healed.

Sometime later, she looked out the window of her filthy cell, and in the distance she saw someone with some bananas, and she began to crave a bite of banana. Everything inside of her wanted one. She could smell them and taste them. Dropping to her knees, she prayed, "Lord I'm not asking you for a whole bunch. . . . I just want one banana. Lord, just one banana."

Then she began to rationalize. How could God possibly get a banana to her through the prison walls? "There was more of a chance of the moon falling out of the sky than of one of (the guards) bringing me a banana," she realized. Bowing her head again, she prayed, "Lord, there's no one here who could get a banana to me. There's no way for You to do it. Please don't think I'm not thankful for the rice porridge. It's just that—well, those bananas looked so delicious!"

The next morning, she heard the guard coming down the concrete walkway. The door opened, and it was the warden of the POW camp who had taken kindly to her. He looked down at her emaciated body and, without saying a word, turned and left, locking the door behind him. Sometime later, she heard another set of footsteps coming down the walkway. The key turned in the lock, and the door opened. The guard threw a huge yellow bundle into the cell, saying, "They're yours!" She counted them. It was a bundle of ninety-two bananas!

As she began peeling her bananas, Ephesians 3:20 came to her mind: *(God) is able to do exceedingly, abundantly above all that we can ask or think, according to the power that works in us.*

She never again read that verse without thinking of bananas. ❧

Topical Index

Scripture Index

If you have an interesting story, we would like to see it! Please e-mail it to pastor@donelson.org, and it may be included in a future edition of *Real Stories for the Soul*. Stories should be between 50 and 600 words and contain fact, not fiction. By submitting it, we will assume your permission to edit and use it should we choose. While we're unable to respond to each submission and cannot guarantee its inclusion in an upcoming book, please be assured we will read and consider every story.

Check your local Christian bookstore for other titles by Robert J. Morgan!

More Real Stories for the Soul
101 stories to challenge your faith and strengthen your trust in God.
ISBN: 1-7852-4517-0

Nelson's Complete Book of Stories, Illustrations, & Quotes
The ultimate goldmine for speakers—humorous, serious, thought-provoking, and heart-warming material. Thousands of real-life stories, illustrations, and quotes indexed by subject and Scripture.
ISBN: 0-7852-4479-4

On This Day
365 amazing and inspiring stories about saints, martyrs, and heroes.
ISBN: 0-7852-1162-4

From This Verse
365 inspiring stories about the power of God's Word.
ISBN: 0-7852-1393-7